MOONTIDES

A Magical Practitioner's Handbook

Wendy Trevennor

GREEN MAGIC

Moontides © *2025 by Wendy Trevennor.*
All rights reserved. No part of this book may be used or reproduced in any form without written permission of the Author, except in the case of quotations in articles and reviews.

Green Magic
53 Brooks Road
Street
Somerset
BA16 0PP
England
www.greenmagicpublishing.com

Designed and typeset by Carrigboy, Wells, UK
www.carrigboy.co.uk

ISBN 978 1 915580 08 22 1

GREEN MAGIC

This book is lovingly dedicated to my wonderful coven and outer circle, for their inspiration, their support and encouragement in all aspects of my life, as well as my publisher, Pete, who is always so encouraging. And to Jessica "JJ" Claydon, who suggested the idea in the first place.

Acknowledgements

My thanks to my good friend Karen Thomas for her care and patience in proofreading and checking my work.
    To Kaff Brooks, author of *Kitchen Table Tealeaves*.
    To Sandie Coombs and Caryl Dailey.
    To Diane Maxey.
    To Janet and Nigel Rome.
    To Mandy Senior.

Contents

Introduction 7

Chapter One: The Physical Moon 9

Chapter Two: Flower, Bird, Wind, Moon 21

Chapter Three: The Man and the Moon 33

Chapter Four: The Inspiration of the Moon 44

Chapter Five: The Guidance of the Moon 55

Chapter Six: The Divine Moon 61

Chapter Seven: The Modern Divine Moon. 81

Chapter Eight: The Moon and Stars 93

Chapter Nine: The Magic of the Moon 111

Chapter Ten: The Protection of the Moon 130

Chapter Eleven: Lunar Healing. 141

Chapter Twelve: The Spiritual Moon 157

Chapter Thirteen: Bringing the Moon into
    Your Practice 173

Introduction

*"Ah, Moon of my Delight who know'st no wane,
The Moon of Heav'n is rising once again:
How oft hereafter rising shall she look
Through this same Garden after me – in vain!"*
   – Omar Khayyam (Edward Fitzgerald translation).

What is the Moon? A big chunk of rock, a pretty light in the sky, the stuff of nursery rhymes, a trashcan for space industry waste, a possible future home for humans, a ball of green cheese ... And yet the importance of the Moon to many people on Earth can hardly be overstated. Through the ages it has been a focus for myth and magic, for art, poetry (it's such an easy rhyme!), and literature, for spirituality, and for science. No one can deny that there is something special about its appearance, the gentle, semi-metallic light it sheds, which is not pure white but delicately tinctured with hints of yellow and pink and may often be brassy or deep red. Its beauty, particularly at the full, and when it seems to come closer to the Earth, is no less than stunning.

The Moon enters our consciousness at a very early age: cot mobiles, nightlights, picture books for very young children, and nursery rhymes all feature serene and smiling Moon faces. Children very quickly come to recognise it and to begin to appreciate its magic, perhaps staring out of their bedroom windows at night when they should be asleep, getting excited in the car on the way home because the Moon is "following" them, sometimes even beginning to understand and anticipate the cycles of this so important asteroid. Fast-forward a few years, and many teens are starting to discover a new fascination with it, as paganism, witchcraft, and an interest in magic grow and spread in our society. For pagans and magicians, the Moon has always held immense significance, as it often has for non-magical people as well. Adults see in it a focus for romance: how many secret trysts between lovers has it seen, how many romantic nighttime picnics, how many marriage proposals? It has inspired poets, painters, songwriters, authors.

When I started this book, I knew I had not taken on an easy job: trying to encapsulate the facts and the immense importance of this astronomical and astrological body in one small book is a challenge. But my remit was to create a single resource that would give as much information as possible to the seeker after knowledge, whether they be a poet or a pagan, a stargazer, or a seeker after general knowledge. I hope I have gone some way towards achieving that.

One final note about the text and the pronouns I have used for the Moon: I started off with "it" in the first chapters, as I was discussing the Moon as an inanimate object, a celestial body. However, as the book grew, I found myself in subsequent chapters having to acknowledge the magic, the beauty, the *personality* of the Moon, and this called for a resounding "she".

WENDY TREVENNOR

CHAPTER ONE

The Physical Moon

*"We've come so far, thought the astronaut
as he swam around the capsule in his third week
and by accident kicked a god in the eye."*
— Rolf Jacobsen

The Moon has many secrets, especially considering that it is the nearest object in space to us. Looking up into the night sky, at the fragile-seeming new crescent, it is difficult to realise that this is actually a ponderous asteroid, more than a quarter as large as the Earth. It measures 2,158.6 miles in diameter, 27.26% that of the Earth. Although, being in space it weighs nothing, if you could lasso it and bring it down on to the Earth's surface then it would weigh in at 81 *quintillion* (81,000,000,000,000,000,000) tons, and would immediately collapse under its own crushing bulk, certainly creating huge damage to the Earth's structure as well. And that astonishing light, that can sometimes be bright enough to wake you, shining through the curtains of your bedroom window? Not its own: the Moon has no light except what it receives from the Sun and that sometimes reflected from the Earth. Another secret is its far side, facing away from the Earth, unseen by human eyes until 1959, when the Russian spacecraft Luna 3 collected images of the so-called dark side (actually it is lit by the Sun just as often as the side facing us). The Moon's orbit and rotation coincide exactly, so that this hemisphere is always turned away from us.

Alexander the Great's childhood tutor, Aristotle, referred to a time "before the Moon." He was writing of the Arcadians, or Peloponnesians who, he said, had seen the birth of the Moon. Aristotle was, of course, normally a sensible chap who knew the Earth was round, and he was employing artistic licence, as of course the Moon is pretty well as old as the Earth, and was in the sky long before any life emerged on Earth. The Moon was born four and a half billion years ago—probably at around the same time as the Earth. Astronomers are divided as to how this happened, but one theory holds that the Earth simply captured a passing object with its gravity, and the two settled down together in an orbital relationship, whilst another idea is that the Earth and Moon were formed simultaneously from dust and debris orbiting the Sun. Two further theories are that either the Earth, as it cooled and solidified from gaseous and molten debris around our Sun, was struck by a large object—which, according to NASA, could have been as big as the planet Mars—which took away a large part of its substance, or part of the Earth was shot out into space due to the speed at which it was spinning and the still fluid nature of its composition. Scientists recently put forward the theory that this impacting object was an ancient planet that, with its stolen piece of Earth, is still present in the Moon's core. They named it "Theia" (the Divine One). Scientists have also speculated that the Pacific Ocean was the site from which this material was taken, creating the world's largest and deepest body of water. Either way, the result was that our planet acquired its enormous Moon—proportionately the largest in size against its planet and the fifth largest satellite in our solar system, which includes moons like Ganymede, which is bigger than the planet Mercury, and the well-named Titan. The Earth is actually quite unusual for a planet of any size in having only one moon—some of the larger planets in our solar system

THE PHYSICAL MOON

have more than 50! The Moon has no satellite, submoon—or "moonmoon"—of its own. This is not as crazy as it sounds: a large moon may well be capable of attracting and holding in orbit a satellite smaller than itself. Saturn's moon Rhea was once suspected of having subsatellites, and it is thought another Saturn moon, Iapetus, had one in the past.

Astronauts have brought back a large amount of Moon dust and rocks over the course of time, but these samples raise as many questions as they answer about the origin of the satellite. If the Moon were taken from the Earth's substance, or both bodies were formed simultaneously from the same debris, scientists would expect to find that it is made of identical material, while if its origins lay elsewhere and it had simply been attracted to Earth's gravity, its substance ought to be completely different from Earth's. Confusingly, the Moon shows a mix of similar and very different materials that do not fit in with most of the theories about its origins, though it may point at the idea of the Earth being struck by another object, which is the favourite theory today.

Slowly, over millennia, both Earth and Moon were shaped into approximate spheres (neither is a perfect orb) as they cooled—just as spinning water drops form near-perfect spheres due to their own gravity, surface tension, and centrifugal force—and the Moon's orbit around the Earth—at a fairly consistent 238,855 miles distance—was established. Were there a speed camera in space, it would record the Moon travelling at 1,667 mph. It also travels, very, very slowly, away from the Earth, moving around 4 cm away from us every year. Its orbit, or lunar year, is 27 days long, and the rate at which it spins on its own axis, the lunar day, is also 27 days, which explains the fact that we only ever see the one familiar face of the Moon, with its well-known "seas" and "ocean". However, the Moon has a third cycle, caused by the intervention of the

Earth itself, which causes the apparent waxing and waning of the Moon, from new to full to waning to dark and back to new again in a 29.5-day period. The part of the Moon that is obscured in every phase but the full is caused by the angle of the Moon to the Earth and Sun.

The Moon keeps to a 29.5-day cycle, which brings the full Moon into the sky at sunset, rising and setting a little later every day, so that by the new Moon, it is rising in the early morning, with the sunrise, and setting in the early evening (like the Sun, it rises in the east and sets in the west). The Moon is in the sky in the daytime as much as it is at night, except at the full and new phases, yet we associate it with the nighttime, and when it is spotted in the daytime sky, people will point to it, as though it were some strange phenomenon. Obviously, it is harder to spot in the daylight, but we seem to feel its appearance then is just a little unnatural. Nor does our satellite rise and set in the same places every lunar day. The positions of moonrise and moonset change slightly every day because of the effects of the Earth's orbit around the Sun and the Moon's orbit around us. In the winter it may rise a lot further north than it does in the summer. The Moon's movements around the Earth are also affected by the Sun's gravity.

If you imagine the Moon starting its cycle at the moment of new, it rises at dawn with the Sun, so it is quite invisible. Within a couple of days, it becomes possible to see a tiny fingernail-like sliver of crescent in the evening sky, as the Moon pulls away from the Sun. Confusingly, the waxing Moon has its points to the left, instead of being a nice, easy-to-remember C for crescent shape. When it reaches its first quarter, the Moon is a semicircle, and after that it is called *gibbous*. When the Moon moves into *opposition* with the Sun, that is, on the opposite side of the Earth, it becomes a full

Moon, which will rise at sunset and set at sunrise. After that the Moon starts to wane until it becomes a crescent again, this time a waning crescent with its points to the right, before returning to darkness after its 29.5-day cycle.

Diagram One: How the Moon phases work

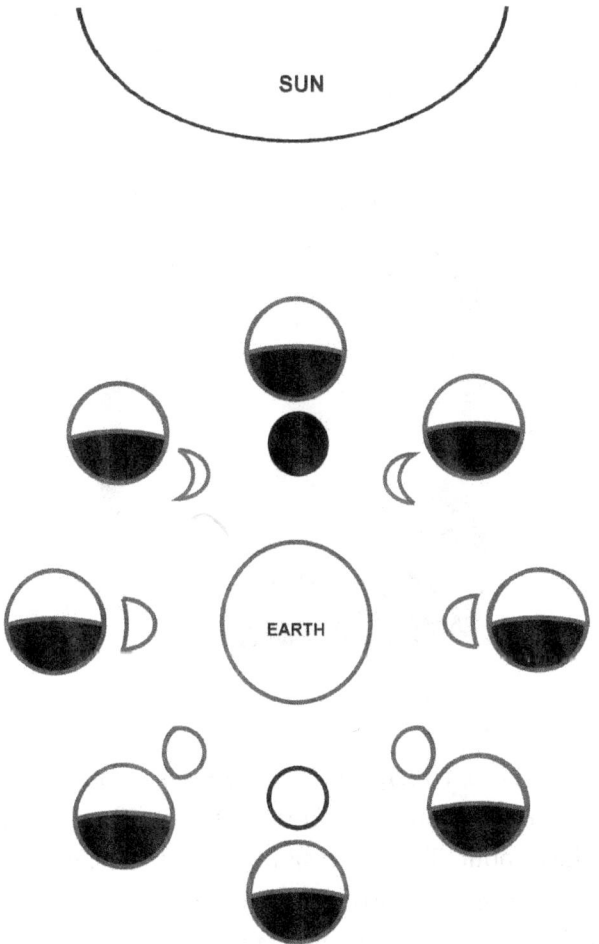

At the dark Moon, the Moon interposes between the Sun and Earth, so that the lit side of the Moon is turned away from the Earth. The Earth is responsible for the two to four lunar eclipses that happen every year. This can only happen at the full Moon, when the Moon is on the far side of the Earth from the Sun, and the Earth gets in the way, blocking the light from reaching its satellite. Another phenomenon caused by the Earth is variously known as "the old Moon in the new Moon's arms" or "the Moon showing her petticoats." Seen from the Earth, the new Moon is bright but holds within its curve the whole of the rest of the Moon, as a dimly lit shape. This is caused by Earthshine and can only happen at the new Moon, when the Moon is between the Sun and Earth.

Diagram Two: The Old Moon in the New Moon's Arms

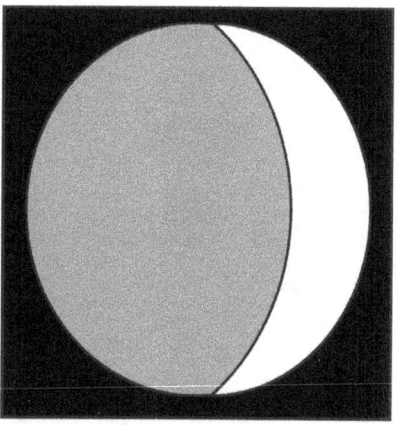

A fourth rhythm of the Moon is the Metonic cycle, discovered by the fifth-century Athenian astronomer Meton, a 19-year period after which the Moon phases occur on the same calendar dates because 235 lunar cycles add up to 19 Earth years—just about. There is a small discrepancy, of only about two hours. There is also a phenomenon known as "lunar standstill" or lunistice, which occurs when the Moon reaches the very northernmost or southernmost point of its orbit against the ecliptic—the central part of the sky. A major lunar standstill only occurs every 18.6 years and has an effect on tidal activity.

THE PHYSICAL MOON

The Moon also affects Earth days. As it very slowly pulls away from us, this gravitational pull slows the Earth's rotation and thus increases the length of a day—by 2.3 milliseconds every century. This might sound infinitesimal, but it is estimated that the first full days—including the light and the dark hours—on Earth were around 10 hours long, so the Moon's moving away has more than doubled the length of our days in the 4.5 billion years since both bodies were formed.

Moonlight reaches us very quickly. Light from the Sun takes 8.33 minutes to reach the Earth, yet its reflected light takes only 1.5 seconds to reach us from the Moon. There is also a very dimming effect, caused by the rough and dusty Moon surface—if it were shinier, we might very well experience 24-hour days at phases when the Moon shines at night, but the Moon only reflects about 10% of the light it receives from the Sun. Moonlight is not pure white but, due to its surface materials and the Earth's atmosphere it has to pass through, it is delicately tinged with hints of lemon and pink, like the precious metal silver, with which the Moon is associated.

Sometimes the full Moon appears much larger and brighter than usual. This is called a supermoon and occurs when the Moon comes closer to the Earth than usual, arriving at or approaching its very closest point to the Earth, which is called "the perigee". At these times the moonlight may be up to one-third as bright again as at a normal full Moon. This occurs because the Moon's orbit is elliptical rather than circular, and supermoons may happen as many as four times a year. The Moon also appears much larger as it rises, due to the magnifying effect of the Earth's atmosphere, which the rising Moon enters at an angle, and it is often coloured red as it rises or sets because of atmospheric gases that filter blue from light—the same reason the Sun appears red as it rises and sets.

Green cheese? Nope, the Moon is constructed in a quite similar way to the Earth, with a core of solid iron, which, like the Earth's, is still molten, and a surface made up of rocks and dust. Like the Earth, its molten core has resulted in volcanic eruptions (though there are no active volcanoes there today), and the asteroid has also been bashed by countless meteors, these giving rise to the familiar pitted look of the Moon. The patterned appearance of the Moon's surface is made up of pale grey or silvery areas of anorthosite, a chalky igneous rock formed during volcanic activity, and which is dusty-looking, while the dark "seas", or maria, are in fact flat plains between higher rocky areas and are darker than the surrounding terrain because they are made of glassy black basalt that flowed into them while molten. The largest are the Oceanus Procellarum (*Ocean of Storms*), which is some 1,595 miles in diameter; the Mare Frigoris (*Sea of Cold*) at 992 miles; and the Mare Imbrium (*Sea of Showers*) at 698 miles. The far side of the Moon has far fewer features, and only around 1% of it is considered *maria*. It is often referred to as the "dark side of the Moon," inaccurately, as the Sun pours light onto the far side as it turns towards the Sun in its orbit. The topography of the Moon also includes mountains, "lakes", "marshes" and "bays".

For a long time, scientists believed it had no atmosphere, but in fact it does have a very thin layer of noble gases like argon and neon, with some carbon dioxide but no oxygen. The thinness of this *exosphere* accounts for the pitted, holey appearance of the surface, as the Moon has had little protection against meteors and other small objects that have hit it over the millennia, unlike the Earth, where the deep atmosphere is likely to destroy any object hurtling towards the surface. Its scant atmosphere is also far too thin to protect it from radiation, so the Moon's surface is charred by UV rays and heat from the Sun and other radiation from further away in space. The Moon also has water, either absorbed into its rocks or lying in its many craters. India's Chandrayaan lunar probe program (Chandra is the Sanskrit word for Moon and the name for a lunar Hindu God), started in 2008, has found evidence of water in numerous craters on the surface and at the south pole of the Moon. It is believed there is also water trapped in rocks. As the surface often reaches well above boiling point, there being insufficient atmosphere to mitigate the direct light and heat of the Sun, much of this water will be vapour some of the time. The rest of the time it will be ice. When not in sunlight, the temperatures plummet to minus 133°C, a good deal colder than the lowest temperatures recorded on Earth, even at the colder South Pole.

Any schoolchild can tell you that the bulk of the Moon affects the water on Earth, causing it to swell upwards towards the Moon as it passes, thus causing the tides of the oceans and other large bodies of water. It also has a significant effect on other natural things, including breeding behaviours in wildlife and flying insects, bats, and bird navigation. Despite this, due to its smaller bulk, the Moon has much less gravity than the Earth, around one-sixth, and to prove it, film exists of astronauts exuberantly leaping and jumping in apparent slow motion on the surface.

It has also had a great effect on mankind, whose natural curiosity as science came into its own was to want to physically travel to the Moon and lay hands on it, take samples, explore, and see whether life was possible on this asteroid. The first manmade object to touch the Moon was Luna 2, an unmanned Soviet vessel that crashed into the Mare Imbrium in 1959 (Luna 1 having missed the target and flown out into space, lost forever). The next projectile, Luna 3, took pictures that allowed mankind to see the far side of the Moon for the very first time. These missions, all in the same year, shattered people's limited expectations about what we could achieve as a species, and before long the USA was getting in on the act as well. Their first space flight was Pioneer 4, which flew past the Moon in 1959 but was off course and failed to record any data.

The USSR continued to hold the upper hand, and the first man in space, Yuri Gagarin, left Earth on 12th April 1961 in Vostok 1, orbiting the Earth once before returning. The USSR also sent the first woman, Valentina Tereshkova, into space in Vostok 6 two years later, but these were simple orbits of the Earth, and soon the program turned its attention back to the Moon. The unmanned Luna 9 achieved the first soft landing on the Moon in January 1966 and also took the very first photographs taken on a body other than the Earth. Luna 10 launched on 31st March 1966 and began orbiting the Moon four days later, making the Soviets the winners in this leg of the lunar "space race." It continued to return information on radiation and gravity for almost two months before its batteries went flat (yes, really!) and it crashed into the Moon's surface, where it remains today, with a growing amount of other manmade debris. It is perhaps better remembered for the broadcast of the communist anthem *The Internationale* from the vessel across space to the 23rd Congress of the Soviet Communist Party. In 1968 the Russians' next venture, Zond 5, became the first vessel to carry life forms—two tortoises, fly eggs, and plants—into space. It flew once around the Moon and brought the animals and plants safely back to Earth.

The US achieved their first orbit of the Moon in 1966 with Lunar Orbiter 1, which sent back data from August to October of that year, including the famed first photograph of the Earth taken from space, showing the Earth as a crescent. Orbiter and Surveyor projects continued to attempt and achieve landings on the Moon through the later 1960s, whilst the USSR was now planning manned flights, experimenting towards this end through their Luna and Soyuz programs.

However, the first manned flight to orbit the Moon was achieved by the USA, with Apollo 8 in December 1968, the mission that brought back the famous colour photograph "Earthrise" after orbiting the Moon 10 times.

Powered by competitiveness as well as carbon powder-based fuel, the Cold War race to the Moon peaked with the first manned landing on the Moon in late July 1969, when Neil Armstrong and Buzz Aldrin left the lunar module, which took them from Apollo 11 to the surface, and walked on the dusty crust of the Moon. At this point the huge financial costs had stalled the Soviet Moon program in its tracks, and cosmonauts never made it into lunar orbit or onto the surface. Armstrong's immortal words, spoken as he set foot on the surface and broadcast across the world, "This is one small step for (a) man, one giant leap for mankind," overshadowed the official inscription on a plaque left behind on the Moon: *"Here men from the planet Earth first set foot upon the Moon. July 1969 A.D. We came in peace for all mankind."* The astronauts also left two medals on the surface; medals awarded to Yuri Gagarin and Vladimir Komarov, who had both died in 1967, Gagarin in a flying accident and Komarov in a Soyuz space capsule that crashed to earth. Twelve people have so far walked on the Moon since that day.

On a less spiritual note, an awful lot of trash has been left on the Moon, sadly human waste, including astronauts' sick bags, toiletries and food packaging, and unneeded equipment and tools—left to lighten the load for take-off back to the Earth. There are even works of art up there. Altogether the amount of material left adds up to a staggering 223 Imperial tonnes, or half a million pounds, the bulk of it being around 70 space vehicles that were left behind as it was too difficult to bring them back to Earth. There are golf balls on the Moon, as Apollo 14 astronaut Alan Shepard had a go at putting while he was there, and Apollo 16 astronaut Charles Duke famously left a framed photo of his family. Six US flags have been planted in the Moon's surface, and there has been one human burial at the time of writing (2024), that of the ashes of Eugene Shoemaker, a geologist who discovered the comet Shoemaker-Levy 9.

In return for what they have left behind, Apollo astronauts have brought back around 850 lbs of lunar dust and rock samples.

As there is almost no atmosphere and therefore no winds on the Moon, one further thing left behind is Neil Armstrong's footprint, which he photographed for posterity. However, with almost every developed nation getting in on the act, questions start to arise about ownership of the Moon. Certainly, the Americans were the first to set foot there, but China (who brought home samples from the far side of the Moon for the first time in 2024), India, Japan, and the USSR have also landed craft on the surface. How long before wars begin over lunar territory?

CHAPTER TWO

Flower, Bird, Wind, Moon

"Flower, Bird, Wind, Moon."
– Zen expression referring to the four senses unhindered by preconception

The effect of the Moon on nature fulfils every magical belief: it moves plants, stimulates animals, herds and guides fish and birds, tinkers with hormones and provokes sex, moves the oceans, and deforms the very shape of the Earth. As it has been attached to the Earth from its very earliest times, it is not stretching matters too far to suggest that the Moon played a vital role in the development of life itself. It certainly plays a part in the protection from cosmic forces of the Earth's surface and the life now extant here.

The effect of the Moon's gravity on the seas is well-known, its passing causing the Earth's waters (and this includes every little puddle, but is only observable in large bodies of water such as seas, oceans, and larger lakes and rivers) to swell in the direction of the Moon, observably rising against land masses. Meanwhile, the waters on the opposite side of the Earth also swell out, an effect caused by the Earth's own gravity and inertia, as the Moon's gravitational pull is far weaker on that side. Thus, both sides of the Earth experience two high tides in every lunar day, plus, of course, two low tides where the

Moon's pull is less. The highest tide of all is that at the full or new Moons, when the Sun's gravity is added to the mix to create what are called spring tides (the opposite of this, called the neap tide, occurs at the mid-point between full and new, the half Moon). The tides are not equal across the world, with the UK seeing some of the greatest changes in sea height at up to 14.5 meters (in the Severn Estuary and Bristol Channel), while on Baltic, Caribbean, and Mediterranean coasts the tidal changes in height may amount to literally nothing. The tides go on to influence weather systems and even affect temperatures at the poles, where the Moon's gravity is known to exert a strong influence on the ice caps and may be a factor in the breaking up of ice masses, due to the stresses caused by its gravitational pull.

But such is the strength of the Moon's influence that the effect is not confined to watery matter. The Earth's crust and mantle are similarly deformed—though obviously not to the same extent—by the Moon's gravity, rising by up to 8 inches (20 cm)! The Earth is a great deal more plastic than our forefathers knew and is also affected by the gravity of the Sun. Scientists also now believe the Moon plays an active part in keeping the liquid and semi-liquid iron outer core of the Earth moving, thus maintaining the magnetic field, the magnetosphere, generated by this movement. This field makes possible all life on Earth by keeping the atmosphere in place and protecting it from the harmful radiation of the Sun. There has long been a theory that the Moon may also play a part in seismic events such as tremors and full-blown earthquakes and even volcanic activity. Although science has yet to come up with any proof that this is so, it is easy to see how the pull of the Moon at its perigee can influence the movement of tectonic plates and even lava flow.

The very air we breathe is manipulated by the Moon, which exerts a cyclic pull on the atmosphere, the winds, weather patterns, and temperatures, including the powerful El Niño and La Niña oceanic events, which are declared when maritime temperatures reach an extreme—warm for El Niño and cool for La Niña. These events exert a strong influence over weather systems and the speed of ocean tides, which extends as far as the US and Northern Europe, by bending the Pacific Jet Stream so it flows in a more southerly direction.

The Moon balances and moderates Earth's weather with its magnetic effect, steadying and mitigating with its gravitational hold the Earth's "wobble" on its axis, which causes seasonal change—without the Moon, these would be much more extreme and the emergence of living things might never have happened. The Moon is now known to create an atmospheric tide that changes air movement patterns and air pressure, going some way towards explaining the observable link between the full phase and electrical storms and other weather changes. Another reason for this may be the Moon's influence on magnetic particles that are always whizzing past in space, but under the Moon's gravity may be attracted to or have their flight paths bent towards the Earth. It is speculated that the Moon may even contribute some heat to the Earth from the Sun's rays reflected from its surface—remember, the sunlit face of the Moon reaches around 121°C, so it has plenty of warmth to pass on, like a space heater close to your legs when you are working in a cold room! Its gravitational pull plucks at winds, clouds, and air pressures, influencing the weather in ways still not yet fully understood. Yet everyone knows there is a correlation between the Moon's behaviour and appearances and the tricks of the climate. While a ring of fluffy clouds around the Moon means rain within a day, a simple "ring around the Moon," or Moon halo—often full of prismatic colours—warns of icy cold on its way, for the "halo" is made up of refracted light shining through ice crystals in the atmosphere. "Clear Moon, frost soon," is another saying on the same theme, and folk have long observed that a winter full Moon brings a long stretch of very cold weather. The Moon "on her back"—with the "horns" uppermost—is said to mean dry weather, as though it holds the water to itself as in a bowl. Conversely, if the points of the Moon face downwards, you can expect rain, and an old belief says a blue Moon (the second full in a calendar month) means torrential rain and floods! A white Moon means dry weather, and a red Moon means rain, goes another adage. This can be explained by the dust—or lack of it—in the atmosphere. In a clear sky the Moon will appear colourless, because there is no dust to colour its face—or for water droplets to collect around. The more dust particles there are in the air, the greater the chance that moisture will have something solid on which to form raindrops, and the dust will also alter the perceived colour of the Moon to a reddish hue. And as if it needed to be any more magical, the Moon can create its own version of a rainbow, called a moonbow. This is rarely seen, as conditions have to be just right: as much moonlight as possible on a dark night when there is precipitation or a nearby source of fine water spray, such as a waterfall. Although they are not made up of white light alone, moonbows are seen by the human eye as pure white.

So much for the Moon's effect on our planet. But it doesn't stop there, as living things across the Earth and in the seas are very much affected by the Moon, sometimes in very remarkable ways. Many types of fish lay their eggs at certain phases of the Moon so that the tides resulting from this will protect their eggs and give their offspring a better chance of survival. Some species, including perch, salmon, and trout, time their mating to the night of the full Moon, and fish that migrate in order to mate are stimulated to do so, both in the seas and in fresh waters. Australian corals—and some corals in other regions—release their eggs and sperm simultaneously in a huge full Moon breeding event in December, an event that can be seen from space. Sea turtles famously arrive on the beaches where they lay their eggs at the full Moon, when they have enough light to see but are less likely to be attacked by predators that might be around in the daylight. The high tide associated with the full also decreases the width of the beach the turtle mothers have to climb before they can make their nests above the water line. Later, after they have hatched, the baby turtles use the moonlight shining on the water like a beacon to navigate their way to the sea. Marine worms that live under the seabed time their mating for the new Moon—how they know when it occurs is anyone's guess. The Moon is also important in navigation for small crustaceans such as sandhoppers and crabs—when you are that tiny, it is important to know which way to go to the sea and safety! The increased light at the full Moon can change fish behaviours in other ways, including feeding.

On land, grazing and hunting animals prolong their feeding cycles under the full Moon, taking advantage of the increased light—though some hunters will be less active as they are more visible to their prey, and it has been observed that lions, which generally hunt at night, will hunt during the day at the full. Wildebeest change their routines according to the Moon's phase, hiding out in safer areas of concealing brush in the darker phases and venturing out boldly when there is plenty of moonlight. These sorts of behaviours are found in many other herd ruminants, while some, such as buffaloes, will gather together in larger groups for safety when the Moon is giving less light. Rabbits and hares, both animals strongly associated in many cultures with the Moon because of the patterning on the asteroid that resembles a crouching lagomorph, sadly do not have an observable special relationship with the Moon, though they may remain inactive on the nights of the full Moon when there is more light for predators to see them.

Canines such as wolves and some foxes, including pet dogs, howl or bark at the Moon (though this may in fact be instinctive behaviour aimed not at the satellite but at nearby members of their species), while birds may become agitated and fearful, and cats may become anxious and hide in odd places around the house, perhaps because they can see activity outside that their humans cannot. One study found that household pets were much more likely to need veterinary care at the full, leading to a 23% increase in visits to the vet, largely for injuries.

Insect breeding generally is stimulated by the full. The Ancient Egyptians associated the scarab beetle, otherwise known as the dung beetle, with the Sun, and yet this large industrious coleopteroid uses the Moon's light to find its way with its ball of faeces—in which its eggs are laid—to a safe hiding place. Without moonlight, the beetle will wander around helplessly instead of travelling in a straight line, making it easy prey for an enemy.

Children's films often feature cute frogs croaking in chorus under the full Moon, and they are right (apart from the "ribbit ribbit" croaking, which British frogs don't do). Frogs and also toads time their breeding by the Moon, getting together at or close to the full. Unfortunately, this also means disaster for many amphibians as they journey, sometimes across perilous terrain, to get to the pond chosen for their romantic encounters, and road deaths for amphibians have been recorded as peaking at the full. Some neighbourhoods organize "help a toad across the road" schemes at the full Moon or at least put up signs asking motorists to be careful not to run the animals over as they cross the tarmac to reach their watery love trysts. On the other hand, reptiles tend to be a lot more diurnal in their habits (being cold-blooded, they need the Sun's heat to remain active), but it has been observed that marine iguanas prefer to make their dives at low tide, which is, of course, Moon-influenced, and when they are about at night, reptiles, especially snakes, are much less active at the full.

In the air, migrating bird species often use the Moon for navigation, sometimes timing their arrival at their destination to coincide with the full Moon, perhaps because their long journey spans nights as well as days, and they need its light to see their way. Owls, which are generally nocturnal, find hunting more problematic at the full Moon, as their prey can also see them, so they spend moonlit nights hooting to one another, communicating, and perhaps seeking mates. Bats, long associated in people's imaginations with the full Moon, tend to avoid it, perhaps because they find its light disruptive, and prefer to rely on their sophisticated sonar system for hunting. Moths are well-known for their tendency to fly into lamps, often to their deaths. The most popular theory for this behaviour is that the insects use the Moon for navigation, steering at an angle to the great light in the sky. But they mistake manmade lights for the Moon, and because these are nearer, they spiral round and round, getting closer and closer, and eventually end up flying straight into them.

If even creatures with brains and the power to move are affected by the Moon, it is hardly surprising that plant life is also deeply impacted. Not surprisingly, sap moves through plants more strongly at certain Moon phases—just as the waters of the Earth move in tides. This may be due to the gravitational effect of the Moon on the plants themselves or to its effect on pulling moisture into the upper layers of the soil, thus bringing water to the plants' roots.

Farmers in all cultures have long used the Moon's phases as a calendar for drilling, mowing, and harvesting, and many home gardeners—even in the UK—similarly keep an eye on the lunar phases, using a different phase for planting, tending, and harvesting flowers, root crops, fruit, and leafy herbs. Older farmers will tell you the water in the fields rises at the time of the full Moon, and this would be the time to plant many types of crops, as the seeds are bathed in moisture from the start. A farmer friend in East Anglia also passed on the tradition that the older farmers of his acquaintance would always go out to catch eels and shoot ducks at the full, as these creatures are particularly active then. Fishermen may plan their nocturnal fishing trips according to the Moon phase, as many believe the fish, especially freshwater fish, are more active and more likely to rise to the bait at the full Moon, whether this is caused by the increased light, the gravitational pull, or some other lunar influence. Some believe that fishing at a total lunar eclipse will be even more successful, perhaps because the fish become disoriented.

The Moon may even affect the food that we eat. Another friend told me that it is a commonly held belief that meat, fish, and other short shelf-life food products will spoil in moonlight, though there is no real evidence that this is so—unless the meat has been left out on a very warm night. As someone who bakes bread regularly, I have to say that the Moon phase does not affect it nearly as much as the warmth in the kitchen, but some people feel the Moon phase does have an effect, a different one according to which kind of flour is being used, so that wheaten bread may do better under a waning Moon and rye bread will rise better under a waxing one. Some pagans plan their cooking and eating habits around the Moon phase, eating nourishing and sustaining foods during the waxing phase, feasting on rich foods at the full, and eating leftovers and generally moving to a lighter diet as the Moon starts to wane. The dark of the Moon might be the right time for an actual brief fast. Alternatively, the waxing and full phases might be a time for sticking to a strict diet and expecting the full Moon energies to cooperate in producing weight loss. Not sleeping well? There is a soothing drink, based on Ayurvedic ideas, in Indian culture called "Moon Milk", which is given to children and adults at bedtime (which presumably accounts for the name). It may be actual dairy milk or milk made from soy, nuts, or other plant materials, which is warmed and then flavoured with spices, including typically turmeric (for its glorious colour), ginger, cardamom, and cinnamon. Sometimes called golden milk, it resembles the old English idea of a posset.

The Moon's supposed constitution of green cheese (that is, cheese that is very new and has not matured to have the desired strong flavour, rather than cheese that is actually coloured green) leads one on to associate it with dairy activities, and it is no surprise to learn that churning butter has traditionally been done at the full. Churning is not as simple as it appears: sometimes the "magic" that turns the milk fat into butter refuses to work quickly—or at all—and there are stories of dairymen dropping a golden or silver coin into the churn to speed up the butter's "coming". In India, ghee is often made under a full Moon, as it is believed the sacred energies of the moonlight will go into the food. Moving on to eggs, whether or not hens lay more or bigger eggs at the full, there is certainly a belief among chicken farmers that the eggs should be set into incubation so that they hatch at the full, as it is believed this will produce healthier and more productive chicks.

Moon phase gardening is a central concept in biodynamics, a system developed a century ago by the Austrian occultist, Rudolf Steiner, in which natural rhythms are used for horticulture. This continues to be popular, and there is even a system for identifying and labelling produce grown according to this method, in the same way as organically grown produce. In the US, a 200-year-old publication called *The Farmer's Almanac* provides full lunar timetables and advice on how to use each phase across seven time zones on the American landmass. Similar publications, including the iconic *Old Moore's Almanack*, well over 300 years old, can be found in the UK and other countries.

Lunar farmers believe that, just as the Moon creates watery and even earth tides, it exercises a similar influence on growing things, which varies according to the nature of the plants and the crops they will become. Lunar farmers and gardeners take note of the four phases of the Moon: new, first quarter (that's the one that is a semicircle or half-moon), full, and last quarter, before planning their horticultural activities. These four phases mark the boundaries between periods that are considered suitable for different types of garden or farm work. The basic premise is that a waxing Moon, one that is growing larger in the sky, is suitable for encouraging plants to grow upwards, while a waning Moon might only benefit underground crops, and the last quarter, leading to the dark Moon, is not suitable for any growing projects.

The timetable works something like this: in the first week of the Moon (that's between the new Moon and the first quarter), above-ground, leafy crops like cabbage, lettuce, spinach, green herbs, and flowers can be planted, as the Moon's energies are pulling upwards towards growth above ground. In the second week, after the first quarter Moon but before the full, plant fruit crops, including tomatoes and courgettes, as the Moon's energies are now directed at ripening and enlarging fruit. In the third week, after the full Moon, the energies change, and the Moon is now pulling towards the growth underground, so plant root crops like carrots and potatoes. In the final week, when the Moon is waning, the system advises nothing should be planted, as these waning energies could blight any crops you put in. So, this is a good time to prune shrubs (as the waning Moon energies will prevent excess bleeding of sap), dig over the ground, pull weeds, and destroy pests—or forget the garden and go away for a holiday!

At the other end of the growing cycle, harvesting may also be ruled by the Moon phase, with a waxing Moon being ideal for cutting leafy plants such as cabbages, lettuces, kale, spinach, and herbs; a full Moon for root vegetables and fruit; and a new Moon being considered all right for harvesting, though not the optimum time. The waning Moon is used for harvesting crops for storage.

The system is further complicated by the astrological sign that the Moon occupies, with certain signs being associated with certain plants and crop types: air signs (Aquarius, Gemini, and Libra) encourage flowers, fire signs (Aries, Leo, and Sagittarius) benefit fruit, water signs (Pisces, Cancer, and Scorpio) boost leafy plants, and earth signs (Taurus, Virgo, and Capricorn) aid root crops. These ideas appear to be based on magical correspondences, a body of knowledge that witches and other pagans use that assigns certain qualities, colours, scents, and influences to the four elements, to planets, and to astrological signs, rather than to any scientific observations. I think I feel one of my headaches coming on, but many people in all parts of the world through the centuries and up to the present day have believed in this and timed their gardening work by it. If you are a pagan, it may well come naturally to you in any case.

As a final idea, why not plant a Moon garden? If you are a reasonably nocturnal, or at least twilight, person, then you will get a lot of pleasure from this idea. A small, enclosed part of your garden could become a magical space for you to work, hold a ritual, or meditate in, especially if you install a comfortable seat. A Moon garden would be composed mainly of white flowers that will gleam under moonlight, of course, but also those that open at night or distil their fragrance at night, such as jasmine, night phlox, tobacco, and some lilies. Many fragrant herbs are also silver, white, or variegated with these colours, such as some artemisias, lavenders, silver thymes, eucalyptus, curry plants, and some varieties of rosemary, whilst many non-fragrant plants like brachyglottis, cineraria, and pittosporum (love these!) have silvery or white foliage that would show up well by moonlight. Smaller bedding plants could also contribute to the atmosphere, grown in among the herbs: Stachys byzantina (lamb's ear), Lunaria (honesty), and the stunning range of large-leaved silver brunneras. The garden would also be a haven for moths, some of which are now quite endangered.

CHAPTER THREE

The Man and the Moon

*"It is the very error of the Moon,
She comes more near the earth than she was wont,
And makes men mad."*
– Shakespeare: *Othello*

The effects of the Moon on the Earth and its waters, on animals, and on the minds and bodies of humans are also mysterious, long suspected, and believed even when unproven, and in many cases acted on even to this day. There is a long history of beliefs in the Moon as a strong influence on human beings, as a cause of madness and violence, an influencer of health and human biological cycles, even a force that might determine the time of human births and deaths.

Probably the best-known belief is about mental illness. Lunacy: the word itself comes from the Latin name for the Moon, which was believed from earliest times to cause or aggravate mental illness and abnormal behaviour in afflicted people. Physicians from the earliest beginnings of medicine linked the Moon phase, especially the full, with increases in abnormal behaviour in persons affected with madness and even with physical ailments, or those now recognized as such, like epilepsy. Hippocrates, the groundbreaking fifth-century Greek physician still known today as "the Father of

Medicine," wrote that "no physician should be entrusted with the treatment of disease who was ignorant of the science of astronomy." This despite his being the first doctor to affirm that illness was caused by natural problems and not curses from the Gods. His opinions were influential throughout most of history, though mentally ill people endured terrible treatment and conditions through the ages, being chained and confined and subjected to unpleasant and sometimes downright brutal or even dangerous "treatments", including beatings, bloodletting, emetics and laxatives, immersion for long periods in cold water, and later on electric shocks. During the Medieval period, under Christianity, madness was regarded as a punishment from God, or alternatively as a form of demonic possession, and sufferers could be tortured or even burned at the stake.

The eponymous Bedlam (Bethlem Hospital in London), not originally founded as an asylum for the insane, kept patients in straw-strewn cells with little food—in common with prisons at the time, they were obliged to buy their food from the staff—and in conditions of utter filth. They were also subjected to being stared at by tourists who would pay to see the inmates, just as in a zoo (no doubt with their scented hankies firmly clasped over their upper-class noses). Accounts say the prison warders had patients chained up and flogged at the full Moon to maintain control. Bethlem Royal Hospital still exists and became part of the South London and Maudsley NHS Foundation in 1999.

The association of the Moon with mental health has long been an accepted fact by the man in the street, and records exist, even from model asylums, of staff leave being cancelled and extra security precautions being taken with dangerous patients at the full Moon. However, the little research that has taken place in recent years has tended to debunk this, seeing no palpable link between Moon phases and increased mental health symptoms, except in the case of bipolar disorder, in which a small-scale study published in 2017 recorded a regular association between the different phases of the illness and those of the Moon in 17 patients. Similarly, no link has been proven between Moon phase and suicides.

However, there does seem to be a link between Moon phase and the symptoms of dementia and Alzheimer's Disease. Many who care for confused elderly people will be aware of the phenomenon known as "sundowning", when towards the evening the person becomes much more confused and also often exhibits challenging behaviour, but Dr. Beck of Purdue University in Indiana, US, found types of behaviours that lasted for longer periods during the full Moon. He focused on the four typical dementia behaviours of anxiety, wandering off, verbal aggression, and physical aggression and found patients exhibited more of these than normal and at higher levels.

Establishing a link between the full Moon and violent crime is problematic, as any increase in crime could be due to factors other than the supposed lunar *influence*, such as increased light at night, which might be considered more conducive to nocturnal crimes such as murder (although it could also be argued that its light might work for the forces of law and order, discovering any criminal who lurked in the shadows with a bloody knife). Any study conducted into a link between the full Moon and human behaviours would have to be done under dense cloud cover. And no, Jack the Ripper did not time his activities for the night of the full Moon—if its light could even be seen through the London "particulars", the choking fogs that frequently cloaked the streets of the city at that time. I was amused to learn that the traditionally accepted belief of an increase in violent crime at the full is known as "the Transylvania effect".

A study conducted into the links between Moon phases and murders in Finland between 1961 and 2014 showed a clear link between murder and the full Moon—but not the one everyone expected. The study showed deaths by homicide were approximately 12% less likely at the full Moon than at other phases (the study divided the lunar month into eight phases). Setting aside the joke that 99% of the findings of studies by scientists agreed with the aims and objectives of the people sponsoring them, there remains a chasm between different sets of scientific findings and also between these and the observations of professionals in their own fields, police officers, hospital staff, and emergency services personnel. Scientists are, of course, very wary of anything they cannot explain or understand, and especially of the slightest whiff of superstition or alternative belief, the association with which could seriously impair their careers.

However, anecdotal evidence tends to favour the original belief, and it is difficult to dismiss the conclusions—and decisions based thereon—of professional people with long experience in their field. And of course, in some cases, due to their numerical nature, statistics are incapable of recording significant information. Sussex Police noted a link between the full phase and an increase in aggressive behaviour and violent crime on the streets, so earlier this century they formed a policy of increasing the numbers of officers on patrol at the full Moon. A friend who worked as a social worker tells me that staff holidays in her department at the time of the full Moon were discouraged, as it was "well-known" that family troubles have a habit of coming to a head at this time. Statistics show no change in the volume of ER activity at the full, yet nursing staff report that, while actual numbers of incoming patients may not increase, the behaviour of the people awaiting emergency treatment—and attending friends and relatives—seems to become more aggressive, sometimes violent, and even bizarre, with more fights breaking out, abuse of staff, sexual mishaps (don't ask!), and odd conduct generally. This may go some way towards explaining the discrepancy between the statistics and the experiences of people in the field: statisticians are generally more focused in their fact-gathering, perhaps on numbers rather than nature or intensity; the experience of people on the ground is rather more all-embracing.

Whether or not links between the Moon's phases and human behaviour or misbehaviour must be classified as folk belief, with little or no basis in fact, there remains the question of how the Moon performs when it comes to human physiology. The most obvious aspect is the female menstrual cycle: is it merely a big coincidence that the average woman's cycle roughly corresponds to the lunar cycle? Again, although women living in close proximity, such as in a single sex college or a convent, may find their menstrual cycles synchronizing, there is no evidence that they correspond with the Moon's phases. A 2021 study of more than 500 women of childbearing age found no correlation between their cycles and the phase of the Moon, and other studies in the past have come to the same conclusion. Menstrual cycles vary by some days, in any case, with cycle lengths from around three weeks to five weeks being within the accepted norm, and many women's cycles being extremely irregular as well. The pioneering biologist, Charles Darwin, suggested that the cycles needed to link to the tides, when human beings lived a semi-marine existence feeding on shellfish and other sea foods that might be more available at low tides, but it is difficult to see why he thought menstruation might affect these food-gathering activities, unless he speculated that the presence of blood in the water might attract sharks.

There is anecdotal evidence that maternity hospitals see an increase in births at the full, but again, there is no *statistical* evidence to back this up… and any astrologer will tell you that the occurrence of a full Moon in birth charts is no more nor less likely than any other Moon phase. Yet a dear friend who, before her retirement, was a midwife tells me, "Full Moons are always a busy time for midwives and births! Especially during the night! In my experience, they were pretty much all natural births, not ones that needed any interventions. Babies just popped out then! Midwives tend to accept that this is a natural occurrence every month." My friend is also a very competent witch, so she would have been aware of the Moon phase at the times she was working. Changes in barometric pressure have been shown to play a part in the onset of labour in some cases.

Studies have been carried out on many aspects of human physical health and their relationship, if any, with Moon phases, which seems to me to be a no-brainer: if our bodies are composed of up to 60% water—and the brain with its plethora of physical, emotional, and intellectual functions, 80%—it seems obvious to me that the Moon's tides and cycles would affect us in the same way they do the oceans and other watery bodies on the Earth. Many people, especially those who follow a nature-inspired spirituality such as paganism, will tell you that they are deeply affected by the Moon's cycles, usually reporting that they are stressed or overwhelmed at the full and feel energized at the new. They may also link their feelings to the aspect of the Moon occurring in their birth charts. Indian people have a strong belief in the association of the Moon phases with ongoing pain levels, such as those caused by arthritis, and will tell you that these grow worse at the full and the new. They may even routinely take extra aspirin or paracetamol pre-emptively on these dates. One elderly friend told me her corns were always worse at the full Moon, and that she would choose an extra roomy pair of shoes, a not-very-fashionable pair she never wore at other times, to wear at this phase. Of course, it is easy for a cynic to point out—with some justification—that the placebo effect might be playing a role in any supposedly lunar-induced symptoms.

However, the most convincing evidence of the Moon's influence on health is its effect on sleep patterns, with many people reporting that they cannot sleep well at the full Moon. An old superstition relates that sleeping under moonlight can lead to all sorts of horrors, including blindness, stuttering, bad dreams, or just plain old bad luck.

Studies show that people do take longer to get to sleep at this phase and additionally take longer to get into the dreaming stage of sleep, known as REM (Rapid Eye Movement), which is vital for human health. People deprived of REM sleep in studies have shown symptoms of psychosis. At the full, the Moon is in *opposition* to the Sun, so it is in the sky for the whole night. Whether the effect is due to the increased light—though a stout pair of curtains would obviate this effect fairly well, and in our modern well-lit towns, it can hardly be a major problem by itself—or some other sensitivity to this phase, research showed that hormone activity displayed distinct changes at the full, with some hormones, such as ghrelin, being lowered and others raised. Ghrelin is a hormone that, among other functions, triggers hunger, so its relative absence plays a part in allowing you to sleep without feeling hunger. People who have just awakened usually experience some delay before they are aware of a need to eat. The body's reaction to the lowering of this hormone could lead to compensatory overeating the next day, which, as we all know, leads on to more of the same and could be the beginning of an obesity problem. The sleep effect was particularly noted in children, who seem more sensitive to the full phase. And the disruption in sleep patterns is also a known trigger for migraines (many people speak of their "full Moon" migraines, saying they are worse at this phase or only occur at this phase of the Moon) and a factor in the development of health problems such as heart disease and diabetes, as well as mental problems like anxiety and depression. At the least, full Moon-induced sleeplessness can lead to a day of headaches and general feelings of unwellness the following day. Sleep deprivation can also lower the immune system, as well as the mood, thus affecting your day-to-day well-being and even leaving you vulnerable to infections and "bugs". It is likely to cause an increase in inflammation, a normal body function that is important to the healing process, but in excessive amounts can trigger diseases such as diabetes and cancer; in fact, a study published in the National Library of Medicine in 2023 showed a marked relationship between the Moon phase and an increase in diabetic symptoms such as neuropathy and oxidative stress (a lack of antioxidants in the body) in type 2 diabetic patients.

However it may affect the quantity of sleep, the Moon seems to have a strong effect on the quality of the experience, with people reporting their strangest and most vivid dreams around the time of the full Moon and in the days leading up to it. British psychologist, Richard Wiseman, author of *Quirkology,* conducted a sleep study of 1,000 people and found, quite by accident, as the study was directed at another topic, that they all reported much more exotic and memorable dreams at this time. As we leave childhood, dreams become much harder to remember because of our busy lives and the lesser importance we give to them, but the more vivid dreams—usually those we dream towards our moment of waking in the morning—do stay in our memories longer. Many people keep a dream diary, writing down the details as soon as they awaken. One simple trick to remember your dream is to concentrate on just one detail, without trying to recall more, and you should find more of the dream's content returns to you.

The Moon has a marked effect on the cardiovascular system, with blood pressure readings observed to fall at the new and full phases. The heart rate can also be lower at these phases, and researchers found that the heart rate would return to normal after physical activity or excitement more quickly at the new and full. Statistics show an increase in heart attacks when the Moon is at its apogee and furthest from the Earth. A study published in 2000 found a strong link between painful attacks of gout and the new and full phases, and there is an observable link between asthma attacks and the new and full, particularly in children.

One study showed a notable difference in the outcomes of patients receiving surgery according to the Moon phase, with recovery faster, less pain and fewer complications in the waning phase. It is a matter for speculation if this might apply particularly to more watery areas of the body, such as the eye. A study published in the *Urology Journal* suggested that kidney problems such as stones could be more painful at the full.

Human sexuality may be affected by the full Moon, and not just because of the romantic atmosphere created by that softly glowing orb in the night sky. Some studies have shown that testosterone production, after falling for the few days beforehand, rises in both men and women at the full, leading to increased desire for sex and more spontaneous erections in men. Whether it also increases fertility in women depends on their own individual cycles and how they align with the Moon phase.

Finally, is there a proposed lunar rhythm for the gut, as there is for planting? I watch my weight (having once been very overweight), and I can assure you that the Moon does have an effect on me. I have been in my target weight range for over five years, but I do notice that the odd pound or three can creep on just after the full and creep off again at the new. To my surprise, I heard this being discussed as unquestioned fact at my slimming club the other day by people who are not pagans and not especially interested otherwise in the cycles of the Moon. Yet they accepted it, both the organizer and several of the target weight alumni, as an established fact that people gain weight or retain fluid at the full Moon and shed it again more easily after the full has passed. To follow a lunar regime, it would make sense to start a diet on the day of the new Moon (been there!) and even to fast at this time, also maybe beginning a new exercise regime, as your energies will be high. As the Moon waxes, it is time to be careful, as you may find every bit of food you eat lands on your hips; your appetite may peak, and by the full Moon you may find you have gained a pound or two during the month. This is the phase at which you will experience cravings for cream buns, instead of the nice, healthy celery salad you had prepared for yourself. I have a hard time avoiding chocolate—well, all the time, really, but especially at this time of the month, and at my age it is no longer anything to do with hormones. The gut may also have a harder time digesting at this phase, and people often report feeling bloated and gassy. But once the moment of fullness is passed, the gut begins to recover from this phase, and the bloating and cravings should disappear as the Moon wanes. This is a good time for a clean-out of some sort, maybe just some Andrew's Liver Salts or other colon cleanse. There is even a Moon plan diet, involving starting a fast on an accurately plotted phase of the Moon. Ex-smokers and recovering alcoholics sometimes report that the full Moon can affect them, making their cravings stronger and increasing their likelihood of giving in to them. I am not a heavy drinker, but I am a frequent drinker of coffee, and I can assert that I drink much more of it at the waxing and full phases and sometimes almost go off the taste of it towards the new Moon. I am, of course, a witch, and always aware of the Moon phase, while many people are not, so perhaps many lunar effects on health go largely unrecognized.

CHAPTER FOUR

The Inspiration of the Moon

"We are all of us wanderers
Chasing moonbeams.
Our hearts full of wonder,
Our souls drowsy with dreams."

– Ramblings of the Claury

*M*onday's child is fair of face ... why is this day of the week called after the Moon in so many modern languages, and not just in English: *Lundi* (French), *Monntag* (German), *Lunedi* (Italian), *Lunes* (Spanish), *Getsuyōbi* (Japanese), *Deftera* (modern Greek), *Chandravara* (Indian), *Mandag* (Scandinavian languages), even *De Luain* (Irish), *Diluain* (Scottish Gaelic), *dydd Llun* (Welsh) and *Dy'lun* (Cornish) in the Celtic languages? The answer seems to be the classical Greek and Roman names for the day, *Dies Lunae* in Latin and Imera Selinis in Greek, which seem to have spread their influence across the world, even into Asian countries. The seven-day week as we know it was officially adopted by the Emperor Constantine in 321 AD and replaced a mish-mash of systems, including a Roman eight-day week. According to which calendar or diary you buy, Monday is either the first or the second day of the week.

THE INSPIRATION OF THE MOON

The man in the Moon is a familiar character from children's stories and nursery rhymes, based on the appearance of a human face made up from the various lunar features visible from Earth. Sometimes he is portrayed as a man having the Moon—with a face—as his head, sometimes as a face formed by the crescent Moon, complete with a nose projecting from the inner surface. The human mind is hardwired to see faces in all sorts of media, from clouds to fire to patterns in soil and trees; this is called pareidolia. Yet the most conspicuous of the Moon's markings resemble a rabbit or hare, complete with two long ears, and once you have perceived this, it is hard to imagine anything else. The creature is made up of prominent surface features, including the Sea of Serenity as its head and the Sea of Tranquillity forming the bases of its ears. It even seems to be sitting on a little scut (rabbit-tail) formed by the Sea of Humours and appears to hold an egg (formed by the Mare Imbrium) in its forepaws. This spectacle has long caused hares to be associated with the Moon (many pagans have a Moon-gazing hare of some sort in their homes or gardens).

Writings and artwork mentioning or portraying the Moon go back to the dawn of time: in some ways the satellite has been more influential than the Sun ... Perhaps because while the Sun is not only hard to look at but also more predictable and prosaic, lighting us and our humdrum activities every day, the Moon is of the night, mysterious, magical, not seen every day, her face marked with strange symbols, her beauty enhanced by the dark blue of the night sky and its attendant starry background, while her ever-changing form excites curiosity.

Perhaps the ordinary person in the street does not pay much attention to the Moon and her doings. They may, if they are old enough, have watched the Moon landings. They may glance at their horoscope in a magazine if it happens to fall open at that page. They may turn over the change in their pockets and mutter "white rabbits" when they first see the new Moon because their grandma used to do this (this was in an era when everyone carried cash ... Do people who still follow this custom today shuffle their bank cards? Or stroke their phone?) But probably the biggest reason for thinking about the Moon is her presence in art and music, not just older pop music of the "June croon spoon" type, but throughout all genres of music from Beethoven to Taylor Swift. The ether vibrates with references: *Bad Moon Rising, Blue Moon, Walking on the Moon, The Killing Moon, Fly Me to the Moon* (the version recorded by Frank Sinatra being the first music played on the Moon in 1969), *Sisters of the Moon* ...

The Moon appears as a cast member in opera and is invoked in many a classical piece, usually as a way of representing the emotion of love and longing or to symbolize feminine or pastoral beauty. She appears in theatre from the earliest Greek dramas, when an actor would carry a crescent banner to represent the satellite, through Shakespeare, and up to the present day. Chaucer, after whom a lunar crater is named, had studied astronomy and used the Moon in mentions and in the plot of *The Franklin's Tale,* when high tides magically conceal dangerous rocks for the lovelorn squire Aurelius. Shakespeare was particularly enamoured of the Moon and mentions her a record number of times through many of his plays, especially *A Midsummer Night's Dream* with its setting of moonlit fairy glades. As a country boy, he must have been familiar with all of her behaviours, perhaps walking home by her light in those days before light pollution. 27 of the moons of the planet Uranus have Shakespearian names, including Ariel, Desdemona, Oberon, Prospero, Puck, and Titania.

In poetry, the Moon may represent divine feminine beauty, or she may speak of old age, illness, or sadness, her pale face seemingly conjuring these states in the minds of many poets. *"With how sad steps, O Moon, thou climb'st the sky, how silently, and with how wan a face!"* wrote Wordsworth, while Shelley asked, in perhaps the most famous poem of all to the Moon, *"Art thou pale for weariness of climbing Heaven, and gazing on the earth?"* The Moon's appearances range from silly children's ditties and nursery rhymes we have all known all our lives, like: *"I see the Moon, the Moon sees me, God bless the Moon and God bless me,"* and *"The Man in the Moon came down too soon,"* verses that may go back many centuries, passed down at generations of mothers' and grandmothers' knees to their children; to much-loved poems like De La Mare's *Silver*. The Moon madness has continued right up to the present day through TV programs our kids—and we ourselves—loved, like *The Clangers, Button Moon, In the Night Garden* (which features a nocturnal Moon-shaped character called Igglepiggle), *Lunar Jim, Mr. Squiggle* (Australia), *Sailor Moon* (for older children and teens), and on to current kids' shows like *Let's Go Luna, Moon and Me,* and *Mr. Moon*. Even Tintin has been to the Moon! The inclusion of the Moon in children's fiction and other media speaks to their sense of wonder and magic, just as the appearance of the satellite evokes deep awe in them when they see it through their bedroom window or the car window as they journey home. Children, and naturally psychic adult people, are drawn to the Moon: I remember my young grandson having a small obsession with her and following his mother around all day saying hopefully, "Moon?"

In visual art, the Moon really comes into her own, the artist empowered by his medium to give his imagination full rein. Any night scene set outdoors naturally includes the Moon, and watery scenes benefit from the effects of moonlight on water. Sometimes stylized (Van Gogh's *Starry Night*), but always glorious and recognizable, she appears in major artworks from the fifteenth-century Jan van Eyck work, *The Crucifixion*, in which a pale gibbous Moon can be seen at the side of the crucified robber Dismas, to the eighteenth-century artist, John Russell, who devoted his skills to a huge number of sketches and paintings of the Moon. The surrealist Salvador Dali imagined the Moon as a city for living in, but also as a huge face watching over a sinister story in one of the most striking representations in his Tarot pack. Gustav Klimt treated the Moon as he did most of his subjects: with imagination, gold, and glitter, while Constable and Turner, both known for landscapes, put the Moon into their work as part of a realistic treatment of a view.

The Florentine Galileo Galilei (1564–1642), the first scientist to study the heavens through a telescope and thus discover that the Moon is a sphere, not a flat disc, was so struck with her beauty and features that he created a set of six watercolour images of the Moon in her various phases. Half a millennium later, an outfit called Foster & Partners is planning 3D-printed bases for people to live in on the Moon.

Movies have long used the Moon—always full and often shown much larger than life—to set the scene for romance, for murder, for a story of haunting or alien arrival—who can forget the iconic image of the little boy and ET on their bicycle, silhouetted against an enormous full Moon? Or the hilarious scene in *Bruce Almighty* where Jim Carrey lassoes the Moon and pulls her nearer to impress his date? Probably the likeliest film to feature the Moon is a werewolf movie, the genre having evolved from the original simple folk tales to include a complex body of lore about these supernatural beings, including their changing into wolf-form for the five nights at and around the full Moon. However, the Moon also makes appearances in vampire films and other horror genres. From

THE INSPIRATION OF THE MOON

Tintin and *Wallace and Gromit* to *Apollo 13*, she has played a cameo or even a starring role in many movies.

In the Marvel Comics-inspired *Moon Knight* series (2022), Oscar Isaac plays the title character, both an innocent museum guide called Steven who loves Egyptology and his alter ego Marc, a superhero who serves the Moon God Khonsu and who wears an astonishing costume made of mummy bandages and a cloak that enables him to fly.

The Moon is also a regular feature of folk tales and nursery stories. As someone who once lived in rural Wiltshire, I was aware of the Moonrakers story, in which some clever country folk get the better of the excisemen after hiding their barrels of contraband brandy in a pond. When they are caught by the excisemen fishing for the goods with rakes, they pretend to be simpletons and explain that they are "fishing for the Moon, as she have fallen in the pond," and point to the Moon's reflection in the water. The excisemen go off laughing at the simple-minded bumpkins, leaving the smugglers to retrieve their prize. This is a tale in which South Wiltshire people take a swaggering pride, calling themselves "Moonrakers". Similar stories about the Moon's reflection in water crop up all over the world, from the cunning Serbian fox who drowns a wolf by convincing him the Moon's image in the lake is a tasty cheese to the Buddhist tale of a band of monkeys who try to fish the Moon's reflection out of the water, holding onto one another in a long chain—until the branch they are hanging from breaks and they all drown.

The Moon has even had a famous single-exhibit event dedicated to her, which continues to tour the world even as I write. Walking into the exhibition entitled *The Museum of the Moon* at Exeter Cathedral a few years ago was a thrilling experience: entering the building, my High Priest and I were met with the spectacle of an immense globe—it is seven meters in diameter, but somehow in that enclosed space seemed much larger—decorated with a perfect facsimile of the real satellite's whole surface, using hi-res images from NASA printed on fabric invisibly stitched together to form a globe. Basically, a giant helium balloon, the sculpture was created by Luke Jerram, who has also created a smaller *Mirror Moon* sculpture in stainless steel and says he was inspired by the dramatic tidal activity of the Severn where he lives. He calls the original Moon "a cultural mirror" for mankind. The exhibit brings its own light and music, but it also invites comment and tribute, and wherever it has gone, at indoor or outdoor venues, it has attracted music, dance, and written responses, not to mention millions of moon-gazers. Another exhibition in 2019 at Denmark's Louisiana Museum of Modern Art included over 200 exhibits using visual art, film, music, architecture, literature, and science put on to celebrate the 50th anniversary of Neil Armstrong's first steps on the Moon.

Moon jewellery, usually in sterling silver or a silver-coloured base metal and sometimes including moonstones or other white crystals, is growing in popularity with the rebirth of paganism—though non-pagans seem to like it too. Earrings, rings, bracelets, hair ornaments, and pendants all feature the crescent Moon, and in pagan ritual it is common to see at least one person wearing a Moon headdress as a symbol of her rank. A very popular symbol among Goddess worshippers is the triple moon, composed of a full Moon disc flanked by a crescent on one side and a waning crescent on the other. Many pagans, and non-pagans as well, sport tattoos featuring the Moon, up to and including diagrams of the full lunar cycle. Moon symbols adorn every kind of clothing—especially children's clothing and nightwear—from underwear and nightwear through to coats and ski clothes, not to mention non-Moon-shaped items like Moon Boots® and Moon Shoes.

In heraldry, the Moon may appear as a crescent or as a full face with human features, usually feminine. The crescent Moon may be *increscent*, that is, crescent, with the points to the left, or *decrescent*, waning, with points to the right, and these two devices may flank the central charge. As a charge on a shield, she is frequently depicted horizontally, with her points uppermost, and may be quite stylized as well. If shown with the points facing downwards, the symbol is called *reversed*. A crescent reversed is also the *cadency device* used on a shield in English heraldry to indicate the second son—who is entitled to bear his father's arms with this addition. The symbol may have been brought into European heraldry by knights returning from the crusades, who had seen it on Muslim badges. A metal crescent-shaped *gorget* was worn by European military personnel from the eighteenth century, forming part of their badges of rank. Deriving from plate armour, it was originally extra protection for the throat, but by Napoleonic times was almost entirely decorative.

Naturally, commerce has got in on the act, and the Moon appears in many company logos, most famously the DreamWorks studios, with its image of a boy fishing from his seat on the lower horn of a crescent Moon. Premier Inns sport a sleepy crescent Moon face that might have come from a nursery rhyme illustration. The iconic American chocolate snack Moon Pie naturally features the crescent on its wrapper. From hotels to restaurants to breweries to food to cosmetics, the Moon is a popular choice in logo art.

In national emblems, the image becomes even more widespread, emblazoning the flags of many Islamic countries and those that are not Islamic as well, always as a crescent (as a full Moon might be confused with the Sun), and often with an attached star. Algeria, Azerbaijan, Malaysia, the Maldives, Pakistan, Tunisia, Turkey, and Uzbekistan are some of the nations with this symbol on their national flag. Not all of them are Muslim countries; the crescent Moon can also be a symbol of a nation that considers itself young and go-ahead.

The English language—and probably many other languages—is full of expressions using the Moon as a simile or metaphor: Moon-faced, mooncalf, over the Moon, moonshine, once in a blue Moon, many moons ago … not forgetting the wonderful term *honeymoon*, which can refer to more than marital bliss and may come from an ancient custom of giving or drinking large quantities of mead at the wedding celebration, or to the supposed sweetness of the first lunar cycle of marriage (as opposed, cynically, to the declining affection of the later years of the relationship). *Moonshine* is a term for nonsense or foolish talk in the UK, whilst in the US it means bootleg or illicit spirits, brewed and sold illegally. "Shoot for the Moon," "ask for the Moon," and "promise the Moon" are popular phrases that testify to her magical preciousness…. No one ever seemed to want to ask for the Sun. On the slightly more negative side, *mooning* is an insulting act involving baring one's buttocks at someone, and *to moon over* something or someone is to act in an over-emotional, silly, or besotted manner. The former clearly takes its name from the round white shape of the exposed behind (though it is presumably used even when non-white people do it), whilst the latter may come from the term "moonstruck", which is a word describing a person acting in this way. "Mooncalf" is another expression that can be used to describe such a person, denoting someone who is simple-minded or totally innocent and originating in an archaic German word for an aborted and malformed farm animal. "Moonlighting" has come to mean taking a second job, perhaps one of which one's primary employer would not approve, whilst "doing a moonlight flit" means disappearing to another location overnight, leaving unpaid rents and other debts.

As well as the Moon Pie, other foods have been inspired by the Moon, most famously the French croissant, a delicate buttery puff pastry that is rolled into a crescent shape. Stories about its origin usually include its being invented to celebrate a Christian victory over Muslim forces. Moon-shaped goodies are also used in paganism: as a coven high priestess, I am sure I am not alone in baking crescent-shaped cakes for the communion-like "cakes and wine" ceremony, which generally concludes a pagan ritual. Moon cheese, Moon drinks and cocktails, and Moon sweets and cakes all pay tribute to her inspiration. There is even a company devoted to producing Moon Steak, vegan "meat".

The Moon can be used on magical equipment in many ways, from simply leaving tools out under moonlight to charge with the energies to painting full Moons and crescents on your altar and its various items. Like many Wiccans, I use a pentacle, an altar tool that sits front and centre and has on it Wiccan symbols, but I also possess a Moon pentacle, a similar item, but one decorated with the full face of the Moon. I created this by simply printing a moon image and sticking it onto a wooden disc, before varnishing it with several coats, but someone with any artistic talent could probably make it from scratch, creating the image with paint.

Why does the Moon appeal so much to us? Why does she inspire so much art, heraldry, verbiage, and entertainment? What is the secret of her allure? The Sun also appears in art and literature but never has the same magical pull. As the Belgian director and novelist Bavo Dhooge remarked, "It's the Moon that moves me. The sunlight makes everything so obvious." It is true that the Moon is the largest and brightest object in the night sky, and in previous generations, she would have been the only illumination for travellers at night. But with our brightly lit towns and cities, our beaming car headlights, and our iPhone torches, this is no longer the case. So, what is it about the Moon? As a witch, I have a ready answer for this, but it is not one that would please everyone, particularly the more scientific-minded. But if you can't accept magic, you cannot deny the beauty and the sheer drama of a huge apricot-coloured Moon coming up through the trees—sometimes at an almost perceptible speed. Tides in human body fluids? Maybe. But maybe my take on it as a witch is just as valid.

CHAPTER FIVE

The Guidance of the Moon

"The Moon has a face like the clock in the hall."
– Robert L. Stevenson

Besides being the Earth's constant companion and benignly influencing Earth rhythms, the Moon generously shares her light, her beauty, and the regularity of her cycles with all. The full Moon rises in the east at sunset, and the satellite rises a little later each night—around 50 minutes later—so eventually she becomes diurnal. A fortnight after the full Moon, the new Moon is still just in the sky during the night, though only visible once she gains enough size to be seen at 48 hours old (24 if you have very good eyesight and live in an area with less light pollution), as she is close to the setting Sun and obscured by its light. The waning and waxing gibbous (that's a Moon that is larger than a semicircle) moons are often seen in the daytime, close to the horizon, if the sky is clear.

Even our ancient ancestors appreciated the Moon's influences and her potential for use as a calendar. The 43,000-year-old Lebombo bone, found in Southern Africa, has 29 notches carved into it, which may be the very earliest physical form of calendar, marking the lunar cycle and carried with its owner, as well as being the very first mathematical device. It is speculated that a woman may have created the tool as a means of keeping track of her menstrual cycle, though it is just as likely to be a simple timekeeper. Ancient hunter-gatherers may have used the Moon cycles to keep track of game movements or just the passage of time, perhaps using the Moon as a "clock" to meet up with others at agreed locations after a certain number of cycles, in a way not possible with the Sun or the seasons. They would also have taken note of the appearance of the full Moon, which allowed them to continue their activities by night, while coastal tribes would have been aware of the influence of the Moon on the tides, helping them to plan their littoral food-gathering pursuits. Some may have used the Moon, as well as the Sun and stars, for navigation or for religious or cultural events. With illiterate cultures, it is not now possible to be certain of their beliefs, though artefacts such as carved symbols, sculptures, and personal adornments can suggest these.

Many later civilisations used the Moon to mark months, though from experience they appreciated that the year had to be based on solar timing, which meant occasionally adding intercalary days so that the calendar did not slip back against the solar year. The Egyptians used 10 months of 30 days apiece, topped up with five intercalary days that had a religious significance (see Chapter Six). Different Native American peoples used 12- and 13-month calendars, while those who used the 12-month method simply inserted an extra month when necessary to stay in time with the solar year. This method was also followed by the Babylonians, who used 12 lunar months (each starting at the new Moon) and inserted an extra month when necessary. Pre-Columbian peoples in Central America used a 260-day year for marking festivals and a more accurate 365-day calendar as well. The shorter year calendar is still used by peoples in some Mesoamerican regions.

THE GUIDANCE OF THE MOON

The Moon continues to be an excellent timekeeper, and in developing countries, it still fulfils the function of a calendar for people who do not yet have the internet laid on in their homes or electricity to power it. Like our ancient ancestors, these people still use the Moon and her phases as a method of marking dates, agreeing on appointments, and setting reminders for agricultural and other work. Even in the UK you can buy lunar calendars to hang on the wall, perhaps designed for pagans or people who practice lunar gardening, or fishermen and mariners who need to know about tides. And while the Moon has influenced the calendars, the calendar influences the Moon: two full Moons or two dark Moons in one calendar month are considered special, especially to magical practitioners, and are called respectively a Blue Moon and a Black Moon.

Modern calendars still use a system based on lunar timings, usually with months approximately 30 days long (in the Gregorian calendar in use across the Western world, these months have been adjusted to fit in with the solar year, so that some are 31 days long and one is just 28 days). The Islamic Hijri calendar consists of 12 lunar months with intercalary days; the Hindu calendar, Panchanga, is a mix of lunar and solar times, as is the Chinese calendar and the Jewish calendar.

Our several times great grandfathers may have used the Moon for more immediate timings; lacking a digital watch, or maybe walking home in darkness too complete to view their turnip watch, they were more attuned to nature than we are today and knew enough about Moon phases to be able to take a rough guess at the time. The Moon was important enough to our forebears that a working display of her cycles was commonly one of the components of the workings of a grandfather clock. From the early eighteenth century onwards, the moon-dial was included in longcase clocks, giving the owner information about whether he could expect a bright full Moon—weather permitting—for any nocturnal travel or work, and also, if he lived near the sea, when the high tide was likely to fall.

It is also possible today to buy Moon clocks and even Moon wristwatches, devices that show the Moon phase without including ordinary time settings. These are sold for sailors and fishermen to help them keep track of tides and nighttime lighting conditions.

The Moon herself can, of course, be used as a clock in much the same way as the Sun, though it is necessary to take note of the phase, and of course she cannot usually perform so well in daylight. Bearing in mind that the full Moon always rises just as the Sun sets gives a good starting point. Actually, it is quite possible, if the satellite is bright enough to cast even a faint shadow, to construct a "moondial" at any phase of the Moon visible during the night. A simple one made of sticks pushed into the ground and a little experimentation can give quite accurate results for one night by measuring the ends of the sticks' shadows, but of course, unlike the Sun, the Moon varies from day to day in where she rises on the horizon. Both objects wander back and forth in relation to the fixed path of the stars, and the Sun's path over the course of a year is called the ecliptic.

Like the Sun and stars, the Moon has been a guide for travellers through the ages, though again a thorough knowledge of her cycles is necessary when using her for navigation. To begin with very simple bearings, the Moon rises, like the Sun, in the east and sets in the west ... though she may wander along the horizon through her cycles according to the time of year and other factors. Another very simple trick to find your bearings with the Moon's help involves holding up an imaginary ruler or any straight edge

THE GUIDANCE OF THE MOON

you have about you (as not many people carry a sextant in their pocket) to the points of the Moon (this obviously will not work with phases that are fuller than the first or last quarter, the half-Moon shape). Take a straight line through the Moon's points and downwards, and that will be south. This only works in the northern hemisphere; if you are south of the equator, the whole idea is reversed, and you are looking for north. The Moon also faces west from sunset to midnight, or rather lunar noon, and east after midnight, if you imagine her as a face looking in a particular direction. When the Moon is at her highest point in the sky, she is due south from Britain … though the most accurate way of working out her highest point will send you back to your Moon-dial sticks to determine where the shadow of the Moon is shortest. A little bit of research before you set out on a night journey to determine when and where the Moon will rise and set will be helpful to you, as you can use this information with the time to see where the Moon is in terms of the cardinal points. It is also useful to look up the time of "lunar noon", when the Moon is highest in the sky, as this will give you the direction of south quite accurately. If you know the time of moonrise and of moonset, you can work out the point of the Moon's highest position in the sky, the point of actual midnight (as opposed to 12am). Say it is midsummer, around the solstice on 21st June, the full Moon would rise at 11pm and set at 4.30am (and remember: at the full, the moment of moonrise will correspond with that of sunset, and moonset with sunrise)—the moment of actual lunar midnight will be 1.40am. This will be when the Moon reaches her zenith in the south. Her face, and any shadows she throws from trees, fence poles, and other objects, will be pointing due north. Of course, one obvious problem is that there may be cloud cover on the night you need to use the Moon for navigation, but it still may be possible to use her position, as the cloud cover may be patchy or the Moon bright enough for you to be able to mark her location. The full Moon directly faces the Sun, so that may also be used for navigation by allowing you to pinpoint the location of the Sun if you are familiar with using it for this purpose. However, this will not be accurate unless you actually have a full Moon to work with and not a Moon that is a day off the full in either direction. The full Moon proper can be identified because she rises as the Sun is setting and is also considerably brighter than the moons on the day before and after the full.

Of course, the most obvious use of moonlight is as illumination – free and no batteries needed! – to navigate at night. With really bright moonlight around the time of the full moon, it is quite easy to walk around with no need for a torch or other lighting, even in woods. Incidentally, I have always been intrigued by the nursery rhyme and song that goes, *"Boys and girls come out to play; the Moon is shining bright as day,"* which dates back at least to the eighteenth century. Was this a reference to pagan ritual or an invitation to come and play with spirits and fairies who were active in the woods at night? More likely it may refer to harder times when children were expected to work for a living and therefore had only the night to play with their friends, at the expense of their sleep quota. There may even be enough light for photography, although, of course, the Moon only gives about one-tenth of the light of the Sun, so the camera exposure settings may need adjusting. However, some stunning images may be captured by moonlight, including landscapes, the sea, the Milky Way, sometimes the Aurora Borealis, and meteor showers.

CHAPTER SIX

The Divine Moon

"The Moon! Artemis! The great Goddess of the splendid past of men! Are you going to tell me she is a dead lump?"
– D.H. Lawrence

How could such an astonishingly beautiful object, afloat in a velvet night sky, fail to stir the spiritual side of any civilisation? This is the chapter I was looking forward to writing, even though I knew it would be a heavy task, as the Moon has been so important through all belief systems…all three of the world's current major religions pay tribute to her. Even the heads of the Christian Church calculate the date of their major festival of Easter via an arcane computation based on the date of the first full Moon after the vernal equinox, which may make pagans smile. In Islam, the deity Allah seems to have a close connection with the Moon, has a crescent Moon as his symbol, and the symbol of that faith generally, and it is speculated by some historians that he may have been a Moon deity—or even Goddess—in ancient times. The Islamic—or Hijri—calendar is lunar-based, consisting of 12 lunar months with intercalary days to keep pace with the solar year. Many belief systems had colourful stories to account for the discrepancy between the solar year and the lunar cycle, as well as to explain the waxing and waning of the Moon disc and also the lunar eclipses. Ramadan, Islam's most important festival, begins and ends with the sighting of a new Moon.

Hinduism also honours the Moon as Chandra, an important deity who is the father of Budha (not *the* Buddha), a deity associated with Mercury.

In Judaism, the Moon was used as the basis for the calendar, said to be based on a commandment given to Moses by God, and "leap months" are added at intervals to straighten the lunar year up with the solar. The new Moon marks the start of each month, and at this time Jews celebrate a monthly festival called *Rosh Chodesh* with religious observances in the synagogue and often a special family meal.

Going back to older civilisations, even belief systems for which the Sun is the major deity tend to also honour the Moon, perhaps as his sister or as a sort of divine accomplice of some sort. Strangely to our way of thinking, the Moon was often a male deity in older belief systems, particularly in Ancient Egypt, where it was represented by Thoth, Set, Khonsu and Aah, while in Central America the Moon could be bisexual or change gender according to its phase. The Moon could also be associated with the land of the dead and its ruler.

Stonehenge is well-known to be a solar temple, but recent thinking is that it also marks lunar events, and at the time of writing it was observed that some of the stones in the outer circle marked a major lunar standstill, an event which happens only every 18.6 years. This happens when the points of moonrise in the south and moonset in the north are as far apart on the horizon as they can get from the ecliptic, with the Moon passing at her lowest point in the sky (unlike the stars, the Moon and Sun do not follow the same path in relation to the equator, and may wander north and south). This happened on 21st June, a few hours after the summer solstice of 2024, and the spectacle was broadcast online by English Heritage, though cloud cover meant it was not very visible in the UK. The impressive Newgrange monument at Donore, County Meath,

Ireland, is oriented so that the rising Sun pours its light down the entrance passage into the central chamber of this huge tomb—older than Stonehenge and in far better condition—at sunrise on the winter solstice, but it is also designed to mark the Moon's 19-year cycle.

Many pagan temples across the world have been oriented towards the east where the Sun and Moon rise, as these rising energies—which come in a tingling wave just before sunrise or moonrise—can be felt in the temples and even utilised in spiritual work. Christian churches also face east, and graves are traditionally laid out facing east as well, due to Christian mythology prophesying that Christ will rise again and return from that direction. Muslim mosques include a praying wall which does not necessarily face east: its orientation depends on where the mosque is situated, as the faithful should be facing Mecca to pray. Similarly, Jewish synagogues face Jerusalem which, like Mecca, is also to the east in the UK.

Crescent moons, often quite stylised, are found in cave art and other carvings left by our ancient forebears, though quite what they mean is another matter. The oldest known sculpture of a Moon-being dates from the Palaeolithic and shows a crescent-shaped human head, possibly that of a female deity. It was found in northern Italy. Many hunter-gatherer tribes seem to have seen the Moon as masculine, and there were often complex myths to explain the waning and dark phases of the Moon and the eclipses.

By the time our ancestors were turning from a nomadic existence to the beginnings of agriculture, the Moon had gained more importance, becoming a benevolent female deity who presided over the growth of vegetation and the increase of animal stock, as well as human fertility and wellbeing. A more representational female figure from this time is the 12,000-year-old Venus of Laussel, a heavy-breasted, broad-hipped nude figure carved on a cave wall, who holds in her hand an object which could be a cow horn (often associated with the Moon because of their shape), but also could be a crescent. She was painted with red ochre, perhaps to represent menstrual blood or the life force represented by blood. If it is a horn, the "blowing" end is turned away from her face. This crescent is also marked with indents or notches which may indicate the 13 lunations of the solar year. She can be seen in the Museum of Aquitaine, Bordeaux.

The oldest civilisations on Earth are, in order: Mesopotamia (from 4,000 BCE), the Indus Valley/Harappa (3,300 BCE), the Ancient Egyptians (3,100 BCE), and Ancient China (2,000 BCE).

AMERICAN (NATIVE)

The indigenous peoples of America marked the Moon phases and had names for the seasonal full Moons, such as Wolf Moon, Cold Moon, and Strawberry Moon, which have crept into use by modern pagans. The Moon herself was "Grandmother Moon", a great spirit who shared the sky with Grandfather Sun, and was generally seen as a symbol of protection, inspiration, wisdom and knowledge. She was also called "the old woman who never dies."

In another tradition, the Moon was bullied and insulted by the Sun, so shrank to a small size and eventually left the sky, returning after she had been comforted by her friends. This makes her compassionate towards anyone who is bullied, and inclined to help them.

ARMENIA

The deity Selardi (or Melardi) is believed to be related to the Babylonian Moon God Sin, but little is known about his or her worship.

The Armenians, who followed a form of Zoroastrianism, also honoured Anahit, a Goddess of war, fertility, wisdom and healing, who was also associated with the Moon. Anahit was a deity of major importance to them, with her consort Aramazd, whose name seems to be synonymous with the Zoroastrian chief God, Ahura Mazda.

AUSTRALIAN ABORIGINALS

There are many streams of belief across the continent, but typically the Moon is seen as male and the Sun as female. In some legends, the Sun is spoken of as pursuing the Moon across the sky. One story describes the Moon as a fat lazy man who was punished for his indolence by his wives, who attacked him with axes and chopped bits off his body. He was finally killed by these injuries, and stayed dead for three days, after which he returned to life and grew fat again. This is clearly the story of the full Moon (the fat man), who decreases in size when he has parts of his body cut off, then he dies (dark Moon), and finally is reborn as the new Moon. In this story, people and animals were all originally immortal, but the Moon cursed them, so that only he remained immortal and all other things eventually perished.

Another strand of belief says that the Moon affects the tides because the high waters run into the Moon as it comes up over the sea, filling it up. As it rises higher in the sky, the water runs out of it, and the tides rise again. A further tale explains the crescent Moon as a magical boomerang thrown up into the sky by an old man.

BUDDHISM

Buddhism was founded some 2,500 years ago, and there are around 535,000,000 practising Buddhists in the world today. The full Moon of the lunar month Magha in the Hindu calendar, is given over to an Asian festival called Makha Bukha Day or Sangha Day, which honours a tradition in which the Buddha enjoyed a festival with 1,250 disciples, on which occasion he told them of his coming death. The event has gained in popularity in recent years, after being promoted by the Thai monarch Rama IV in the nineteenth century. Regular full Moon beach parties, known as Koh Pha Ngan, are also held every month in Thailand, events at which merry-making, fireworks and alcohol play a significant role. I am informed these are also very popular with the young, who enjoy social get- togethers with their peers for drinking, meeting romantic partners and, sadly, sometimes drug-taking.

CELTS

The most obvious Celtic Moon Goddess would seem to be the Welsh Goddess Arianrhod, as her name means "Silver Wheel", yet many other Goddesses were also associated with the Moon. Arianrhod's story seems to have little to do with the Moon; she births two children while stepping over a threshold (thresholds and all kinds of boundaries both physical and temporal were deeply significant in Celtic belief), one of them Lugh or Lleu the Sun God, to whom she petulantly refuses to give a name until tricked by the sorcerer Gwydion. The other is Dylan, who goes to live in the sea, perhaps a reference to Arianrhod's Moon and tidal connections. To the Celts, the circumpolar stars were *Caer Arianrhod* (Arianrhod's Seat), or *Caer Sidi,* a larger section of the sky which produced the Northern Lights. Rhiannon, a Welsh Goddess associated with horses, fertility and diplomacy, and Rigantona, a British Goddess associated with Epona, were also seen as Goddesses of the Moon, as was Cerridwen, a Welsh witch Goddess whose story has her adding ingredients into a magical cauldron for a year and a day, and ultimately giving birth to the divine bard Taliesin.

In Ireland, the chief Goddess called the Morrigan may have been a Moon Goddess, especially likely as she was one of a triad with her sisters Macha and Badb. Irish legends also have a Moon God, Elatha, leader of the Fomorians.

In Briton, the tribal Goddess Andraste, or Adraste, was a war Goddess but also a lunar deity to whom the hare was sacred. Because of this, the eating of hares was taboo to the Celts.

A male Celtic God associated with the Moon is Cernunnos, a very ancient God of woodlands, animals, and shamanism who today is revered by neopagans, sometimes as Herne, though this usage probably owes a lot to the 1980s TV series *Robin of Sherwood*, which featured an elusive godlike woodland figure who acts as a mentor to Robin. The best-known ancient image of Cernunnos is that on the 2,000-year-old Gundestrup Cauldron, a magnificent silver vessel that portrays him in a cross-legged meditation pose and surrounded by animals. More modern representations often show him with a crescent Moon lodged between his antlers.

CENTRAL AMERICA

Aztec belief holds yet another story to "explain" the lesser light of the Moon as compared to the Sun. The Aztecs believed that the Sun was just the latest in a long line of solar Gods who had lived and died. When the last one passed away, the Aztec Gods gathered to decide who should be next to ride across the sky and they prepared a large fire to burn the chosen candidate to make him immortal. Two Gods, Tecciztecatl and Nanahuatzin, both volunteered for this honour, but at the last moment, Tecciztecatl showed hesitation, while Nanahuatzin courageously leapt into the fire. Tecciztecatl then repented of his timidity and followed him, but as there could not be two suns, the other Gods, angry at his cowardice, threw a rabbit at Tecciztecatl. This turned him into the Moon God, with lesser light and a rabbit outline on his shape. The Aztecs also honoured a Moon Goddess called Metztli or Metzi, and a Goddess named Coyolxauhqui, who led her brothers in an attack on their mother, the Earth Goddess Coatlicue, when they discovered she was pregnant, which apparently brought shame on their family. However, her child was miraculously born fully grown and armed and stopped the attack, killing Coyolxauhqui and throwing her severed head into the sky, where it became the Moon.

In Mayan belief, the Goddess of the Moon was called Ixchel and was concerned with women's matters, including home crafts, pregnancy and childbirth, fertility, healing, weather, and war. She could be a fickle Goddess who brought ill luck as well as good.

THE DIVINE MOON

CHINA

In ancient Chinese belief, the Moon Goddess Chang'e, or Heng'e, became immortal (again) by stealing and then drinking a magical immortality elixir, a story that has many versions throughout Chinese literature. In the most classical version, Chang'e is the beautiful wife of a famous heavenly archer called Houyi, who is tasked by the Jade Emperor with sorting out his ten rebellious sons, who have turned themselves into blazing suns. Houyi is so moved and angry by the damage they have done to the Earth and its animals and people that he exceeds his brief and shoots nine of them dead, leaving just one Sun to provide the right amount of light and heat. Demoted from immortal status and banished by the Emperor for this act, Houyi and his wife travel to the palace of the Queen of the West, a Goddess who has a secret elixir of immortality. She gives this to Houyi, telling him that half of the dose will be enough to give him eternal life, while all of it will turn him back into a God. Chang'e finds the drug and, in a moment of temptation, consumes it all (or, in another version, has to swallow it to keep it from being stolen by an enemy), which turns her back into a Goddess. Banned from heaven, she travels to live on the Moon with her pet rabbit (or in some versions a pet hare).

The Chinese still celebrate Chang'e at their mid-autumn festival at the full Moon of their eighth month—which falls roughly between our late September and early October—with lanterns and special food, particularly Moon cakes. They also have a popular superstitious saying that pointing at the Moon can bring you bad luck because Chang'e doesn't like it, and if she feels disrespected, she might cut off your ear! Similar festivals take place across Asia today. The Chinese also celebrate a separate lantern festival on the first full Moon of the New Year, which falls in our month of February, and they have taken this tradition across the world so that it is celebrated in many countries. In Korea, a similar festival called Daeboreum, or Great Full Moon, is held at the New Year, as is Tet Nguyen Tieu in Vietnam, while in Japan a festival called Koshogatsu was once held at the New Year but is now neglected in favour of the Western 1st of January.

EGYPT

The importance of the Moon as a means of marking time was especially relevant in Ancient Egypt, which had, like other civilizations, a calendar made up of 12 lunar months of 30 days, which was then topped up with intercalary days to ensure it kept pace with the solar year. Egyptian belief evolved and shifted over the three millennia of this civilization, with the ibis-headed Thoth being the earliest Moon God, though he later took a different career path and became the God of Wisdom and Knowledge and was associated with the judgment of the dead. His role was later taken by the youthful Theban God, Khonsu.

Whoever the current Moon God was, he was seen as travelling across the sky in a huge supernatural barque during the night, just as the Sun God travelled across the daytime sky in his golden boat. When the Moon barque reached the horizon, it continued on through the underworld, fighting off the monsters and evil spirits in that realm until it reached the eastern horizon and rose again into the sky—a mirror image of the Sun barque's cycle.

Thoth and Khonsu took an important role in the evolution of the Egyptian calendar, supplying the five intercalary days to make up the year from its twelve 30-day months. The legend says that the Sky Goddess Nut and her brother, the Earth God Geb, fell in love, incest being a common theme in ancient creation myths. The Sun God Ra and/or their father Shu were displeased by their marriage and laid a curse on it, saying that Nut could not give birth on any day of the year. Desperate as her belly swelled to enormous proportions, she appealed to Thoth for help, and he challenged the childlike Moon God Khonsu to a game of *senet*, a board game similar to draughts or checkers, winning from him enough light for a total of five days, on which Nut could give birth to her children Osiris, Isis, Set, Nephthys, and Horus the Elder. This legend also explains why the Moon is much less bright than the Sun.

The lunar job later passed to Aah or Iah, a God who resembled Khonsu and was identified with both him and Thoth, but other deities were associated with the Moon as well, particularly if they were Gods of the underworld, such as Anubis and Osiris (who was also linked to the Moon through his continual cycle of rebirth and regeneration). The Goddess Isis was not originally a Moon Goddess but a Goddess of fertility, magic, wisdom, and the afterlife. Possibly a sky Goddess in early times—she has wings in many portrayals—by Ptolemaic times her role had expanded, and she had become associated with the Moon, as well as the sea.

GREECE

By 600 BCE, the Greek mathematicians and astronomers were aware that the Moon was a sphere and went around the Earth. Aristotle said that the satellite was made up of the four humours: earth, air, fire, and water, with the addition of a fifth called *quintessence*. The Greek Goddess of the Moon was

Selene, the daughter of the Titans Hyperion and Theia, and sister to Helios and to Eos, the Goddess of the Dawn. She was seen as driving her silver chariot across the night skies, drawn by two white horses, and wearing a crescent Moon, points uppermost, on her brow or in her hair. In later times, she was conflated with the Goddess of the Hunt and the Wild Places, Artemis, who was a virgin Goddess (in contrast to Selene, who was in love with a shepherd called Endymion). Where Selene was seen as the sister of Helios, the personification of the Sun; Artemis was seen as the twin sister of Apollo, the Sun God. The Greek Moon Goddesses also included Hecate, and modern pagans have seen this as a Maiden-Mother-Crone triad. Artemis represented the Moon on Earth, Selene the Moon in heaven, and Hecate the Moon in the underworld. The Phrygian Goddess Cybele had a crescent Moon and star emblem. She was later adopted by the Romans, who retained her emblem as the badge of the city of Byzantium, which later became a Muslim symbol after the Ottoman Empire captured Byzantium. She is still honoured today as the patroness of the football club Real Madrid, who dress her statue with scarves to celebrate a win. The Goddess Bendis was honoured at Thrace as a variant of Artemis and was seen as a Goddess of hunting and the Moon; though where Artemis was seen as chaste, Bendis kept company with satyrs and maenads.

The Greeks believed that dreams came to sleeping people through the Horned Gates, false dreams through the gate of ivory and true dreams through another made of horn. It is likely this metaphor is connected with the Moon, given the mention of "horns" and the fact that dreaming and sleeping are nocturnal activities.

THE DIVINE MOON

HINDUISM

To the world's 1.2 billion Hindus, the Moon God is called Chandra (Sanskrit for the Moon), or sometimes Soma, and it is fair to suppose that he is honoured across the world, as the Indian Diaspora has taken Hindu Gods to many other countries. Chandra—after whom the Indian lunar program *Chandrayaan* is named—seems to have been a God born to be a trouble magnet. He abducted his lover, a star Goddess named Tara, from her husband Brihaspati's house and made her pregnant with the God Budha. However, the Devas forced Chandra to give her back again. He then married the 27 daughters of a creation God called Daksha, who insisted that Chandra must love all his wives equally. However, Chandra favoured a wife called Rohini and incurred the jealousy of the other 26 wives, who complained to their father that he neglected them. Daksha then placed a curse on Chandra so that he became ill and lost a lot of his brightness.

In another story, the waxing and waning of the Moon is accounted for by Chandra's having incurred the wrath of the elephant-headed God Ganesh after laughing at him as he returned from a party drunk and full of food and vomited after falling over (in sanitized modern versions he is simply carrying the food in a pouch and spills it when he falls). Ganesh threw one of his tusks at Chandra, injuring him and causing a huge hole in his body—presumably the Mare Imbrium—and cursing him so that he would never be whole again. Later he forgave Chandra, and although he could not remove his original curse, he modified it so that the Moon may be seen whole and bright once a month. But because of this curse, it is considered inappropriate to look at the Moon during Ganesh's autumn festival, Ganesh Chaturthi.

The God Shiva, known as *The Destroyer*, is usually depicted wearing a crescent Moon on his headdress. This is a symbol of enlightenment.

INCA

While archaeologists tend to think of the Incas as sun-worshippers, the Moon Goddess Mama Killa, or Mama Quilla, had almost equal importance to them. Temples were aligned so that the Sun and Moon could appear in doorways and windows at certain festivals, and the Moon was used to calculate the dates of these festivals.

Associated with wealth, women's cycles, and marriage, Mama Killa was the wife and sister of the Sun God Inti and was able to weep tears of silver.

Other Moon deities included Quniraya, a Moon God who seems to have been a rather perfidious character. He disguised his sperm as a lucuma, or eggfruit, and gave it to a chaste virgin Goddess called Kawillaka, who then became pregnant and bore him a son. Kawillaka did not know who the father of her son was, so she took him to a gathering of the Gods and asked the father to step forward and acknowledge him. No one answered, so she set her little son on the ground and told him to seek out his father. Quniraya, meanwhile, was sitting at the back due to his lesser rank, but when the baby discovered him, he climbed on him playfully, thus marking him out as his father. Kawillaka was appalled to discover such a nobody was the father of her son, and she fled away to the sea and turned both herself and her baby into rocks.

Quniraya also raped the elder daughter of a God called Pacha Kamaq, who he blamed for Kawillaka leaving him, and would have raped the younger daughter as well, but she outthought him and turned herself into a dove and flew away.

THE DIVINE MOON

INDUS VALLEY CIVILIZATION

The South Asian peoples known as the Indus Valley Civilization, or Harappa, lasted for two millennia from 3,300 BCE, but little is known of their religious beliefs or practices. They built no great temples, although the genital symbols known as yoni and lingam appear to have been revered, and their writing has yet to be deciphered. The yoni, the depiction of the female external reproductive organs, has been associated with the Moon in some cultures.

INUIT

For the Inuit, the Moon was also a male God called Tarqiup Inua or Aningaat. The first name means "Master of the Moon," and he had the Sun as his sister. The Inuit saw the two deities as chasing one another across the sky after a complicated incident involving incest, with the Moon creeping into his sister's dark tent at night and taking advantage of her. Horrified at the rape, she smears soot on her face, as she knows her attacker will return, and she wants to know who was responsible. Sure enough, she is attacked again, and she then follows the man out into the village, where her brother is revealed as the culprit because he has some of the soot on his face. The story ends with a chase across the sky. The Moon's dark markings are explained by the soot.

JAPAN

In ancient Japanese belief, the Sun Goddess Amaterasu has a very uneasy relationship with the Moon God Tsukuyomi-no-Mikoto, to whom she was once married. According to one story, their estrangement causes them to avoid one another, hence the Sun being in the sky during the day and the Moon at night. According to another story, he pursues her across the sky in an attempt to win her back.

KUSH

Due to its close proximity to and its conquest by Egypt, this ancient kingdom was greatly influenced by their religious beliefs and practices, and their pantheon included a God called Aqedise, who was the Kushite version of the Egyptian Moon God Khonsu.

However, unlike the Ancient Egyptians, the Kushite peoples honoured Moon Goddesses, including the lunar and sky mother Amesemi, wife of the lion War God Apedemak. Two lioness Goddesses were also honoured as lunar deities: Miket or Mekhit, also a war Goddess, whose legend sounds very similar to that of the Egyptian War Goddess Sekhmet, and Mehit, a more relaxed-sounding Goddess usually shown as a lioness lying down.

MESOPOTAMIA

In Mesopotamia, the Moon God Nanna (Sumerian) or Sin (Babylonian/Assyrian) was one of the very oldest deities, his worship spanning nearly four millennia. He was also known as Enzu, Lord of Wisdom, and father of the Sun God Utu-Shamash by his wife Ningal. His other children were Ishtar/Inanna, the Goddess of Love associated with the planet Venus; Ereshkigal, Goddess of the Underworld; and Ishkur/Adad, God of Storms. He is generally represented as a man wearing the crescent Moon on his headdress or on the top of his staff and is sometimes portrayed as the king of the Gods. The Great Ziggurat of Ur, an impressive temple structure near modern-day Nasiriyah in Iraq, excavated in the early twentieth century, was dedicated to him. He was a beneficent God associated with fertility and was the protector of mankind. Through his daughter, Ereshkigal, Nanna became associated with the realm of the dead and was later considered as a judge of the dead to whom it was possible to pray for the souls of relatives and friends who had passed into that realm. The cult of Nanna continued in Syria into the third century CE.

The Hittites, an Indo-European people who moved into Asia Minor and lived in the area that is now Turkey some 2,000 years BCE, worshipped Moon Gods, including Arma and Kasku. The latter was the subject of a ritual carried out to appease stormy weather, as he is believed to have been toppled from the sky and drenched with rain by the angry storm God Taru before other deities came to his rescue. Arma, or Ermma, was believed, despite his gender, to watch over pregnancy and pregnant women.

NORSEMEN

Mani, the Norse Moon God, was male and was seen as driving a chariot across the sky, accompanied or followed by two children called Hjuki and Bil, who may have represented or been associated with visible features on the Moon's surface. Mani himself is the brother of the Sun Goddess Sol, or Sunna. Sadly for Mani, another follower is the supernatural wolf Hati, the son of the giant wolf Fenrir and grandson to Loki. Hati and his brother Sköll pursue the Moon and Sun across the sky until Ragnarök, the end of the Gods, when they will devour them.

PERSIA

Little is known of the very early Persians, or Medes, as they left no written records, but it is supposed that they followed an early form of Zoroastrianism.

The later Achaemenid Empire, formed by Cyrus the Great in 549 BCE, honoured a Moon Goddess called Mah, though sometimes she appears as a male God called Mao. She was associated with wealth, fertility, water, and the rhythms of the year but was not a very prominent deity in Zoroastrian beliefs.

PHOENICIANS

The Moon Goddess Tanit, also associated with sex, fertility, and war, was the most important deity in the Phoenician pantheon, along with her consort Ba'al Hamon, a God of fertility and agriculture. There is archaeological evidence that children were sacrificed to them.

Even today in Tunisia it is customary to invoke "Mother Tangou" or "Tannou" in an attempt to provoke rain in times of drought, and the name Tanith is still given to girls. As Phoenician, like Egyptian, was written without vowels, her name may have been Tinit or Tanat.

ROME

As in Greece, there was originally one Goddess associated with the physical Moon, but it later came to be associated with other Goddesses. Luna was the original Moon Goddess, but her territory was invaded by Diana, the Goddess of the Hunt, the Roman version of Artemis, and the queen of the Gods, Juno, was also associated with the Moon. Many of the classical

Greek stories associated with their Gods and Goddesses were adopted by the Romans, such as the love affair between Selene and Endymion, and applied to their own deities. Luna, who is also depicted in Roman art driving a chariot—though hers may be drawn by oxen rather than horses—was also associated with fertility, pregnancy, agriculture, and weather. As with the Greek Moon Goddesses, the Roman ones were arranged in threes, in this case Diana (the new Moon), Luna (the full), and Hecate (the waning and dark). Selene, or Luna, Diana, Artemis, and Hecate are all honoured by modern pagans.

SHEBA

The ancient kingdom of Sheba, or Saba, in the region of modern-day Yemen, worshipped a Moon God called Almaqah who wore a bull's horns and was associated with vines, which are also indicators of his being a Sun God. Almaqah was considered the male counterpart of Shamash, the Sun Goddess, and as the progenitor of the ruling dynasty.

SLAVS

Devana is the name of the Moon Goddess in ancient Slavic belief and seems to align with Artemis/Diana in that she is also a Goddess of nature, fertility, forests, and hunting. Her name also seems to mean "young maiden", which is also close to the way these Goddesses were seen, and she was often paired in ceremonies with Morana, who seems to have been a crone Goddess of death and rebirth.

In Siberian folklore, the dark markings on the Moon are seen as tooth-marks left by a terrible black-winged monster called Alklha, who nibbles at the Moon every night until it disappears from sight altogether. However, it does return every month, as Alklha, who represents the night sky, vomits up all the pieces again.

In more recent times, the strange and terrifying folklore figure called Baba Yaga does have some of the attributes of a Moon Goddess, including her association with female magic and female rituals, but is otherwise really a bogeywoman given to eating people who come across her.

VOODOO

The major Haitian Vodou Loa Erzulie, who has many aspects, is associated with the Moon and is usually represented as pale-skinned, although she originally comes from the ancient western African kingdom of Dahomey. Erzulie is not really a Goddess: most of the spirits worshipped in the 17 or so major streams of Voodoo are *Loas* (pronounced *Lwahs*), that is, spirits that may once have been mortal but have become something much more powerful.

In Yoruba, the major Orisha, Yemanja or Yemaya, a Goddess of the sea, is also associated with the Moon and is seen as the spirit of moonlight and mother of the other Orishas (equivalent to Loas in Haiti). Yemanja emigrated from Africa to the New World with African slaves and is important in modern Candomblé and Umbanda beliefs as a protectress of women and especially pregnant women. Like Erzulie in Haiti, Yemanja shows strong elements of syncretism with the Christian Mary: slaves denied their own beliefs often used imagery from their enforced Christian worship for their private devotions to their own proper Gods.

CHAPTER SEVEN

The Divine Moon Today

*"I, who am the beauty of the green Earth,
And the white Moon among the stars."*
— Doreen Valiente: *The Charge of the Goddess*

The importance of the Moon to modern pagans can hardly be overemphasized. She sits enthroned in the sky—and in their spiritual beliefs—as the Queen of Nature and the Mistress of Magic. Witches and pagans have a kind of doublethink with regard to the Moon; as people raised in a modern education system, they know it is a big lump of rock orbiting the Earth, whilst at the same time seeing her as the face of the Goddess and planning their lives, certainly their spiritual and magical work, by her cycles. As there are just under 13 lunations in a year, the number 13 is special and lucky for witches. The crescent Moon, or Triple Moon, is almost as universal as an item of pagan jewellery or a tattoo, as is the pentagram. They also see the Earth as the Goddess, but this does not appear to interfere with their apparent Moon-worship (actually, pagans do not worship the Moon herself; they simply observe and honour her as a symbol of the Great Goddess).

WICCA AND WITCHCRAFT

In Wicca, depictions of the Goddess, who may have one or several names, some of them secret and used only in circle, are usually bound up with the Moon. She may be shown as a woman wearing a crescent Moon on Her brow, or as a much more abstract symbol made up of circles (the dancing Goddess, often worn as a pendant), but will usually have a crescent Moon about Her somewhere. Most people are aware of the name *Aradia* for the Wiccan Goddess, a name which is used in Wiccan and other pagan traditions across Europe and the US, although it is not one of the secret names by which She is known in some traditional covens. A popular Wiccan chant used in circle and for magic goes: *"Moon, moon, shining bright, Midnight on the water, Oh, Aradia, Diana's silver daughter."* The name goes back at least to Leland's *Aradia, Gospel of the Witches* (1899), an influential book written from Leland's friendship with a Tuscan witch named Maddalena, and seems to originate in the name Herodias, the wife of Herod in the Bible. Aradia is a prophet Goddess, sent to Earth by her parents Diana (the Moon Goddess) and Lucifer to bring enlightenment and magic to mankind.

However, many covens will use other names for the Goddess and God, choosing from every pagan source from Ancient Egypt to names from Shakespeare; Hecate, the triple Titaness from Greek legend, being particularly popular for the Goddess.

Witches associate the Moon and its phases with the "life cycle" of the Goddess, seeing the new Moon as the Maiden, the full as the Mother and the waning/dark as the Crone. This last term, which sounds quite opprobrious to non-pagan ears, describes and celebrates an older woman, one who has passed the menopause and moved into her power as a wiser older woman. Some female pagans over a certain age (often 60) undergo a *croning* ritual to mark this.

I have always had a slight problem with shoehorning the Goddess into this three-phase view of the Moon. The Moon has many phases, not just three, and even at a basic level surely has five: new, waxing, full, waning, dark. I find it easier to equate the Moon's cycles with the whole, naturally flowing lifetime of a female Goddess, who is born, reaches maturity, ages and finally dies, to be reborn again.

However, returning to traditional pagan mores, the colours associated with the phases and the associated aspects of the Goddess are white or silver for the new, red for the full (think of harvest moons) and black for the waning/dark. In Gardnerian and Alexandrian Wicca, these colours are used in the three degrees of initiation. First Degree denotes a priest who has a certain amount of knowledge and wishes to dedicate him- or herself to this spirituality, a little like confirmation in Christianity. White is the colour for First Degree, the colour for the new Moon and new beginnings, and an initiate may be given a white cord belt to wear, though not all covens have the same traditions. Second Degree initiation denotes someone who now becomes a high priest(ess) as they have demonstrated sufficient knowledge and ability; Second Degree priests can perform certain ceremonies, such as handfastings, and may found and lead their own coven with support from the mother coven. The colour for Second Degree is red, the colour of the full Moon. Third Degree is the highest rank in Wicca (people styling themselves "King of the Witches" or other such titles have no sanction to do so) and is associated with the old or dark Moon and the colour black. A Third Degree high priestess may be recognised as such in ritual because she wears a belt braided from her black cord and the red and white ones she received earlier in her training—or a garter made up of these colours in skyclad (nude) traditions. A male high priest would generally wear a simple black cord in token of his rank (or perhaps a metal bracelet or armband with the Third Degree sigil on it).

The God too is associated with night rather than day, though He may be seen as a Sun God. This may be a leftover from the Burning Times when witches were forced to conduct their religious rites in secret, perhaps in the middle of the night in some very distant rural place (and I have to insert a disclaimer here, that not all pagans believe in the Margaret Murray theory of "the Old Religion" surviving underground for centuries under Christian oppression, but may see modern paganism instead as the revival and reclaiming of an ancient but lost tradition).

Modern paganism is all about cycles and the Wheel of the Year, which would have been calculated by our ancestors by the movements of the heavenly bodies. Nearly all modern pagans celebrate eight Sabbats in the year, the quarter days of Ostara (Spring Equinox), Litha (Summer Solstice), Mabon[1] (Autumn Equinox), and Yule (Winter Solstice), plus the cross-quarter days of Imbolc (early February), Beltane (May Day), Lughnasadh (early August), and Samhain (Halloween). The quarter days have clear astrological markers—that of the Sun entering into a new sign, so that the Sun entering Capricorn marks the Winter Solstice and Yule. The cross-quarter days of Imbolc, Beltane, Lughnasadh/Lammas and Samhain do not have universally agreed dates. Some traditions follow the Celtic tradition of the "threshold" of the month, celebrating on

---

[1] This name for the Autumn Equinox was made popular by the American occultist, Aidan Kelly, but it has recently declined in popularity and use. Mabon ap Modron is a character in Welsh myth, associated with King Arthur, and does not seem to have any connection with the equinox.

the last day of one month or the first day of the next, using modern Gregorian calendar dates, and often in any case holding the ritual on the nearest weekend, due to the difficulty for working members of attending on a weekday. However, in some traditions the Sabbat dates are calculated by the Moon. *Lunar* Beltane may be several days after the calendar Beltane, which occurs on May Day and the previous evening, while still other pagans may observe them at the halfway mark (15°) of the astrological sign in which they occur.

These festivals all have their own traditions and correspondences and are generally celebrated with an open ritual and usually a feast or other social gathering. Spread out at roughly six-weekly intervals throughout the year, these mark seasonal changes and are all very different in character. Some are for celebrating the regreening of the Earth as spring arrives, others for planning and aspirations, for gratitude for harvest, or for sorrow and remembrance, all manifestations of the life cycle of the Goddess and God, embodied in nature. Spring Equinox? Celebrate with images of hares and rabbits, with painted eggs and yellow spring flowers. Samhain (Halloween)? Get out the black candles and the photos of your loved ones who have passed away, for the beginning of the dark, cold months is a traditional time to remember them.

Pagan witches also meet for a ritual called *Esbat* once a month, usually at the full of the Moon, although some covens meet on the new. Although they may meet at other times for other purposes, including meditation, tutorials, ad hoc magical work, work to help members of the community, and just social interactions, the Esbat is their regular time for worship. The Esbat relates to the Sabbats in the same way that Sunday churchgoing relates to Easter and Christmas in Christianity. However, for coven members, the Moon ritual of Esbat is the most sacred and also secret, open only to inducted coveners and maybe the occasional well-vetted guest, usually a candidate for induction into the group.

At Esbat, the Goddess is honoured in Her most powerful aspect, the Mother, who is associated with the full Moon; while, as we have seen, the new Moon is the time of the Maiden Goddess; and the old or dark Moon is for the Crone Goddess. These three aspects are seen in spiritual traditions across the world and throughout time: many Goddesses are seen as triple, or three individual Goddesses may be tied together: Persephone, Demeter, and Hecate; the Morrigan, Macha, and Badb; Sarasvati, Lakshmi, and Parvati, while some Goddesses were seen as triple by themselves, such as Hecate, Hera, and the Irish Goddess Bride or Brighid.

At Esbat, a priestess, usually an experienced one, may be the subject of a Wiccan mystery called *Drawing Down the Moon,* in which the high priest of the coven uses certain words and gestures to draw down the spirit of the Goddess into the priestess. Afterwards, she may not remember much, if anything, of what she said or did while channelling, but it is common to hear personal messages for coveners struggling with personal life problems or general messages of inspiration, or the vessel may simply feel a need to wordlessly hug each coven member. If she is Third Degree, it is also traditional to recite *The Charge of the Goddess*, a beautiful, poetic piece of prose written by the Mother of Wicca, Doreen Valiente (1922-1999), around 1960, which is unarguably the most important sacred text in Wicca and which is learned by heart by high priestesses at Third Degree.

Traditional witchcraft—by which I mean *the old ways,* cottage witchcraft as opposed to covenry—also makes use of the Moon in a major way. There is a feeling among all witches and most pagan magical practitioners that moonlight is magic, and most of us would agree that magic works best at night and in moonlight. Every practitioner of magic learns sooner or later to be aware of the phases of the Moon. They may become so attuned to them that they instinctively know, without looking at an ephemeris, when these fall and may look or go outside because they feel the full or the new is happening—and be proved right.

DRUIDRY

Astrology, and also the Moon, was important in ancient Druidry, according to Roman writers who met and interacted with this Celtic priesthood. Both Julius Caesar and Marcus Tullius Cicero met and talked with a Gaul called Diviciacus (though this was a Latin rendering of his real name, which is lost). According to Cicero, Diviciacus was not only a Gaulish king but also a high-ranking Druid with whom he had long discussions on spiritual matters, including divination and astrology, an art at which the Druids were preeminent. Although the Druids were not, as many people believe, the builders of Stonehenge and other such Sun monuments, which were erected in the Neolithic Era, they would almost certainly have used them for ritual (and still do today) and as "calculators" of astrological events that, according to Roman accounts of the time, were heavily reliant on the Moon and her cycles. Julius Caesar wrote that a Druid's training took 19 years, which, as we have seen, is a complete cycle of the Moon, after which it returns to its exact points of rising and setting from 19 years before. The Druids kept an oral tradition, passing their secrets from priest to priest and not writing them down for fear of discovery, so we cannot be sure exactly how they used this information, but we believe they used the phases of the Moon in much the same way pagans and lunar gardeners do today. The ancient Celts also used a lunar calendar (many pagans today use the Ogham Tree Calendar, but it should be borne in mind that this is a modern construct, created by the *White Goddess* author, Robert Graves, in the twentieth century, and does not have any genuine ancient pedigree).

There is an account of ancient Druids performing their famous ceremony of harvesting mistletoe in the writings of Pliny the Elder, the first-century Roman historian. According to him, the Druids did this on the sixth day of the new Moon—strangely, as the plant was associated with Sun-worship. However, the actual ritual does seem to mingle Sun and Moon symbolism. He wrote that the Druid who was to cut the plant (which is a parasite growing in the branches of certain trees, in this case always the oak) climbed the tree, wearing white garments and carrying a golden sickle. Were the white clothes worn in honour of the Moon? The gold metal of the sickle would seem to indicate the Sun, while its shape conjures the crescent Moon. The priest cut the sacred herb and threw it down, and it was caught below in a white cloak or sheet, as it was not supposed to touch the ground, or its magical importance would be compromised. Two white bulls or cows (again, of a Moon colour) were then greeted and thanked before being sacrificed at the foot of the tree. I was surprised to learn that the gathering of mistletoe, which I have always taken to be a Sun ceremony, also includes so much of Moon correspondences, but I was less surprised after doing some research into modern Druidry.

To sum up the beliefs of modern Druids is difficult. I am fortunate to have a "Dru-witch" in my coven, a seasoned OBOD member with whom I have collaborated before. She tells me, "Ask 20 different Druids how they work with the Moon, and you'll get 20 different answers!" She and a fellow Druid, both highly trained and experienced OBOD members of many years' standing, were kind enough to share some information with me on how Druids see the Moon.

Druids, as is well-known, work with the Sun: their rituals and ceremonies are based around solar events, and yet…both were aware of the 19-year lunar tradition and stated that this is very significant in Druidry today, to the point where seeing the number 19 sparks an awareness in a Druid, in the same way that 13 does with a witch.

The Druids also observe the Eight Sabbats, have their own names for these festivals (the quarter days of Alban Eilir, Alban Hefin, Alban Elfed, and Alban Arthan, and the cross-quarter days of Oimbolc, Beltane, Lughnasadh, and Samhuinn), and may celebrate them for a longer period, of up to five days. But while Wiccans generally accept the Gregorian calendar dates for the cross-quarter days of Beltane, Lughnasadh, Samhain, and Imbolc, not seeing them as having an astrological marker, the Druids celebrate these at their lunar markers. So, Imbolc (1st February for a Wiccan) would be celebrated at the full Moon in the sign of Aquarius, Beltane (30th April or 1st May) at the full in Taurus, Lughnasadh (1st August) would take place at the full in Leo, and Samhain (31st October) would be celebrated at the full in Scorpio.

Working with the Moon is a part of individual spiritual and magical practice among Druids, who use her very much as witches do, observing lunar timings for magical workings, the gathering of herbs, and the cleansing of tools and crystals, but also for personal and group meditations carried out at the new and full, particularly the internationally-attended full Moon meditation for peace, which happens every month, led by the Anglesey Druid Order. Many Druids also practice lunar gardening and use the Moon in magic for change, renewal, and transformation, as well as setting intentions at the new.

Like Wiccans, they see the phases of the Moon as Maiden, Mother, and Crone manifestations. Certain aspects of Druid rituals are associated with the Triple Goddess, such as there being three parts to a ritual: the opening, the central ritual, and closing down.

Most Druids are pretty savvy about astrology, and the astrological position of the Moon—as well as her phase—is also taken into consideration when magical work is being done. One of my friends, who comes from the Sami tradition, told me she also observes the Moon's shadow, as in her tradition one's shadow holds one's story, so it is customary to dance within it. My other friend mentioned that much shamanic work is done at the full Moon, with shapeshifting being done by those who are trained for this. Shapeshifting is a spiritual exercise ... no one actually grows hair and starts howling, but a shift does take place within the individual that empowers or inspires them.

The Druids also honour Moon Goddesses such as Arianrhod, Cerridwen, and Rhiannon (who is also connected with the underworld) and see Triple Goddesses as connected with the Moon, just as Wiccans do. Cerridwen has special significance because of her pivotal role in the legend of Taliesin, which is so important to Druid belief. Cerridwen, who is clearly a Crone Goddess who may once have been a Moon deity, becomes the mother of the divine Bard Taliesin through a magical accident. In this legend, the witch queen is brewing a magic potion for her son Morfran, who was born hideously ugly, hoping to imbue him with inspiration and wisdom to compensate for his looks. This involves gathering magical herbs by the Moon for a year and a day and stirring them into an ever-bubbling cauldron, which is tended by a blind man and a boy called Gwion. As the brew reaches its completion, Gwion is splashed on the hand as he tends it. He puts his hand to his mouth—

and the power of the brew goes into him, giving him all the knowledge and inspiration meant for Morfran. Cerridwen, returning at that moment, realizes at once what has happened and that all her hard work has been for nothing. She pursues Gwion with murder in her heart, but his new magical wisdom tells him he is in danger and also how to escape. They both take the shapes of different animals during the chase, but she finally captures him while in the form of a hen (he having taken the shape of a single grain hiding in a heap of corn) and swallows him. However, nine months later, she gives birth to the immortal bard Taliesin, and he is such a beautiful child that she cannot bear to destroy him, so she leaves him to be adopted by the bard Elffin ap Gwyddno. *Taliesin* means "shining brow"... Is it too big a jump to suggest that this connects him to the Moon, also a universal source of poetic inspiration?

One of my friends then drew my attention to the infamous slaughter of the Druids on the Isle of Anglesey by the Romans in 60 CE and told me the isle was at that time called Ynys Mon but was also called Mona, which may be merely the Roman rendering of Mon or may be an ancient word for the Moon. This event holds a sad and special importance for today's Druids, much as the sorrow of the witch burnings does for modern witches.

HEATHENRY

This is a broad term for neopagans who honour the Norse and Germanic Gods, including Odin or Wotan and Thor. Many streams observe the Eight Sabbats, in common with Wiccans, Druids, and other pagans, but some do not. As we have seen in the last chapter, the Norse Moon God was called Mani and was male. The Moon is used in establishing the beginning of the Heathen festival of Midwinter, which starts on the first full Moon after the new Moon which follows the winter solstice, so that it is never less than seven days after the solstice. Some Heathens may carry out magical or ritual practice at different phases of the Moon, but this is not central to the tradition.

THELEMA

The occultist Aleister Crowley (1875–1947) claimed to have been contacted by a spirit named Aiwass while in Egypt, and that this being dictated to him *The Book of the Law*. The philosophy he founded as a result was Thelema, a movement based on Ancient Egyptian beliefs, the central concept of which is the following of one's higher or true will, supported by the two affirmations, *"Do what thou wilt shall be the whole of the Law"* and *"Love is the Law, Love under Will."*

Thelema's most important deity is Nuit, based on the Ancient Egyptian Sky Goddess Nut. Nuit is also a sky and lunar Goddess, portrayed as a naked woman with her body covered in stars. Lunar cycles and energies are used in Thelemic ritual and magic.

A final word about the Moon's influence on matters of spirit is that many paranormal researchers believe paranormal activity is increased at the full Moon, perhaps because the spirits can somehow access the stronger lunar energies to manifest themselves. Others believe the Moon's perigee, her lowest point in the sky and closest to Earth, encourages ghostly activity, so presumably a supermoon, which combines both events, would be the best time to go on a paranormal investigation.

CHAPTER EIGHT

The Moon and Stars

"What if that mystic orb
With her shadowy beams,
Should be the revealer at last
Of my darkest dreams!"
— Bliss Carman

Astrophysicists may scoff, but astrology is the slightly wacky cousin of astronomy, for it depends on studying the movements of the planets and other heavenly bodies. As a pseudoscience, it has a pretty impressive C.V. going back to Ancient China, Ancient Egypt, the Mayans, and Babylon. I have to admit that I have always taken it with a pinch of salt big enough to bring on hypertension, and yet.... As a witch, I have studied it because it goes with the territory, and it impacts on so much of what witches do. Having a ritual and need people to call the quarters (this is a small invoking ritual done at each cardinal point to call down the protection and blessings of the four element Lords, of earth, air, fire, and water)? Many priestesses will ask volunteers what star sign they are, then allocate them a quarter based on whether they are a fire sign, a water sign, an air sign, or an earth sign. An Aries, for example, might be sent off to the south point of the circle to invoke fire, while a Capricorn might be sent to the north to invoke earth. See chart below.

Studying astrology takes a lifetime, but the basics are generally acquired over time by anyone working magic or running a coven or other pagan circle. The ancient stargazers noted that the Sun and Moon, the stars, and the planets appear to travel across the Earth from east to west—this "track" of the Sun is called the ecliptic. Some bodies move more than others, and the circumpolar stars, called Caer Arianrhod (the Seat of Arianrhod) by the ancients, hardly appear to move at all, which is why many streams of paganism treat the north as the most important direction, setting up their altars in that direction. As they move, all at different rates (and yes, I am aware that it is the Earth that moves, not the heavens), they interact with one another, forming *aspects*. When two bodies come close to one another, from the viewpoint of someone standing on the Earth, this is called a *conjunction*, while the opposite phenomenon, of the two being as far apart as they can get against the ecliptic, is called an *opposition*. In between there are trines, squares, semi-squares, sesquares, sextiles, semi-sextiles, and quincunxes, all formed by a planet making a certain number of degrees to another—always, of course, from the Earth. The ten planets in astrology are the Sun, the Moon, Mercury, Venus, Mars, Jupiter, Saturn, Uranus, Neptune, and Pluto, and these have "personalities" according to the classical deity after whom they are named, so that Mars brings energy and even aggression, Saturn imparts a depressing and negative influence, while Venus will flavour the chart with beauty and romance.

The Moon's phases are taken into consideration as well but are identified in a different manner, so that the new Moon is called a *conjunction with the Sun,* the full is an *opposition with the Sun,* and the other phases are squares, sextiles, and so on.

A "snapshot" of these planets is taken for the drawing up of a personal birth chart, and the relative positions of the planets and other influences, such as the horizon and the midheaven, are studied, taking into account the exact time and date and the geographical location of the birth. An experienced astrologer can then draw up a set of indications as to what type of person the subject may be. Astrology does *not* predict the future, just future possibilities based on personal tendencies indicated in the chart. The chart can also be *progressed* to follow the changes in the subject's life so far and compared to the chart of a potential partner to see whether the relationship might work (this is called synastry).

The 12 signs of the zodiac are each ruled by one of the planets (and these have changed historically, so that these past influences also need to be noted). Thus, each star sign has a "personality" based on, or at least heavily influenced by, its ruling planet. These qualities are drawn from classical mythology and the Gods associated with various stories and behaviours. Thus Leo (the Sun = Apollo) is charming, authoritative, generous, creative, courageous, and bold; Virgo (Mercury = the messenger of the Gods and God of Knowledge) is straightforward, conscientious, a bit OCD; Pisces (Neptune = the God of the Sea) is dreamy, intuitive, and artistic; and Taurus (Venus = the Goddess of Love) is warm-hearted, gentle, placid, and loving (Taurus means the bull, but to my mind this sign is better thought of as a cow). The interpretation of the signs also takes into account the form of their name, so that Libra (the Scales) is diplomatic, just, and able to see both sides to every argument; Gemini (the Twins) is said to always be in two minds or even have a split personality, while Sagittarius (the Archer) gets straight to the point! These sign features are also influenced by the element associated with them: as you can imagine, Leo is a fire sign, so has a fiery, bold, active personality, while Virgo is a practical, down-to-earth earth sign, Pisces is a water sign, affected by emotion, and Libra is a slightly wishy-washy, indecisive air sign. The odd one out is Aquarius (the Water Carrier)—not only *not* a water sign, but it hardly seems influenced by its artistic form at all, but rather by its ruling planet Uranus, as a classical God, the father of the Titans. The composer Holst called this planet *The Magician* in his *Planets Suite,* and this is a good way to remember the planet's "flavour". Aquarians are very much their own people, maybe slightly wacky, out of tune with others, *odd,* and magical.

The signs are also assigned an element, based loosely on their name. The four elements, or humours—fire, water, earth, and air—are important in much pagan belief and ritual. No, we don't think we are back in the sixteenth century, but we do see the physical world as being ruled by elemental kingdoms, which are influential in so much of what we do, from calling quarters to spellcasting to divination. And if you think about it, these elements align perfectly with the states of matter: solid, liquid, gaseous, and plasma.

There is a further level of meaning based on whether the sign is *cardinal, fixed,* or *mutable.* These give some qualities to the chart: cardinal implies an inspired or driven person, fixed hints at an inflexible, controlling subject, while mutable means flexible.

Here are the full qualities of the 12 zodiac signs. Note that the start and ending dates of the signs vary year by year and are determined by the date at which the Sun moves into that area of the sky, usually around the 21st of the month.

The sign the Moon is in should ideally be taken into account when performing magic, whatever the phase. So, if you were to want to do a love spell, for example, you would try to arrange it for a time when the Moon was in the sign of Taurus or Libra, both of which are ruled by Venus, the Love Goddess. If you were looking for protection during travel, you would go for a sign ruled by Mercury, so Gemini or Virgo, while if you were up in court and hoping for a positive outcome, you would

Zodiac Sign	Dates	Ruling Planet	Element	Modality
Aquarius	January – February	Uranus	Air	Fixed
Pisces	February – March	Neptune	Water	Mutable
Aries	March – April	Mars	Fire	Cardinal
Taurus	April – May	Venus	Earth	Fixed
Gemini	May – June	Mercury	Air	Mutable
Cancer	June – July	Moon	Water	Cardinal
Leo	July – August	Sun	Fire	Fixed
Virgo	August – September	Mercury	Earth	Mutable
Libra	September – October	Venus	Air	Cardinal
Scorpio	October – November	Pluto (and Mars)	Water	Fixed
Sagittarius	November – December	Jupiter	Fire	Mutable
Capricorn	December – January	Earth	Earth	Cardinal

go for Sagittarius, which is ruled by Jupiter, who oversees all administrative and judicial proceedings. For a fuller explanation of this concept and of the related *planetary hours*, see the next chapter. The astrological details from a person's birth chart might also be used in spellwork, in the same way that a photograph or nail clippings or hair, or even their social media presence, might be used to anchor the identity of the subject, for example, in a poppet (magical doll).

THE MOON IN THE CHART

In astrology, the Moon represents your psychic side, your soul, or perhaps your natural instincts—the things you might think, say, or do from the heart, without thinking and without the intervention of the ego. She speaks of your habits and your home background, your heritage and ethnicity. So, her sign is at least as important as your Sun sign (though some astrologers believe your *rising sign*, the sign that was coming up on the eastern horizon as you were born, is even more important). The Sun and Moon are the major planets, and their effects are generally in a higher gear than those of the other planets. When they appear in their own sign as well—Leo for the Sun and Cancer for the Moon—they become *exalted;* that is to say, their effects are even more powerful. They are always considered *personal planets,* that is, of primary importance in the chart as defining core personality. They also confer this quality on the planets that rule the sign in which they themselves appear, so that, if, for example, your Sun is in Taurus, the ruler of that sign—Venus—becomes a personal planet as well.

The Moon speaks of instinct and intuition, of your inmost self, and she does this through all the signs, so that if, for example, she is in Leo, this would speak of the tendency to be a natural leader, to spring into action without thinking, when a situation arises that needs a positive response. Whilst in Pisces, the Moon might indicate a person who is the opposite, who lives in a dream and naturally reacts slowly and dreamily to any situation. The Moon in Scorpio will bring out that Scorpio jealousy, an instinctive reaction the person cannot help, while in Capricorn the Moon brings a lack of confidence that may even manifest as unfriendliness. This sort of knee-jerk reaction in any sign is the Moon's influence, where the Sun is connected more closely to the person's self-image, the persona they may have carefully constructed for themselves and by which they wish to be known. This sounds like empty vanity, but it is an integral part of the personality and the way most people cope with the pressures of living in the world and with society.

The Moon rules the sign of Cancer, a cardinal water sign. The Moon has always, of course, been closely associated with water, and the sign being cardinal also implies inspiration. In her own sign, the Moon is exalted in her influence, making that sign still stronger. The symbolism of Cancer is a mixture of lunar influences and the supposed nature of seagoing crustaceans ... So Cancerians are said to be emotional and intuitive, even psychic, but also very fond of their homes (that would have to mean the symbol creature is a hermit crab, presumably). They are also supposed to be sensitive, empathic, protective, and cautious and to have very changeable moods. Another piece of astrological lore says that people with a certain birth sign will have some kind of physical marker: thus Cancerian people may have a round "moon face" or moon-white hair (actually, I have known Cancerians who do!).

A further detail of the birth chart is the *houses,* which are divisions of the chart into 12, which may be all the same size (equal house system) or divided by other means. Each house represents an area of the subject's life, such as career, health, relationships, education, travel, and social life. The Moon rules the fourth house, which is all about home and family, not just your current domestic arrangements, but your ancestry and genealogy, your future descendants, your hometown, your inherited possessions, and even your social life and social values. Finding the Moon in the fourth house in a chart obviously means the influence of both is exalted, and much more importance is then given to the fourth house and its concerns.

Returning to the phases of the Moon, the new and full will also have an impact on the birth chart, although they are not identified with these terms. The new Moon (which is described as *conjunct the Sun)* takes on the colour of the Sun sign to a greater extent, making the core personality closer to the projected personality. Of course, the whole business is then further complicated by nearby planets, especially if they are involved in the conjunction, and the Sun and Moon may not be in the same sign either, despite being conjunct (in the case of these major planets, a conjunction may be considered to be up to 10 degrees apart). In contrast, the full Moon (described as *in opposition to the Sun*) brings a potential conflict between the Sun's sign and that of the Moon, which may or may not be strongly felt, depending on the signs themselves.

Astrology takes many years to master, and there are easier ways to use the changing influences of the Moon and other bodies; for which, see the next chapter.

DIVINATION

The Moon continues her journey from the heavens and across the divination methods of many cultures—for who could neglect to include such a magical and striking part of our universe? Divination systems usually include a number of symbols on stones, tiles, staves, or cards, which are selected randomly or thrown onto a cloth or the ground, and the results analysed. Commonly the symbols include the Moon, which is usually associated with magic, intuition, dreams and, of course, female persons.

CLEROMANCY

This is a general term referring to the practice of casting items, whether they be dice, stones, bones, or randomly selected objects, to determine the outcome. Some practitioners assemble a collection of items that may include crystals, bones, coins, feathers, and even quite modern objects like watch faces, and assign each a meaning within the cast. The Moon (as a moon-shaped pebble or other item) may certainly be one of these objects. For its meaning, see the meanings given for the Moon through the systems below.

I CHING

This is an ancient Chinese system already established throughout the country by 300 BC, but probably considerably older. The system consists of *The Book of Changes*, a body of 64 short texts or chapters, each attached to a hexagram made up of six-line patterns, and each delivering a piece of wisdom. The choice of the hexagram to be read is determined by ascertaining the six lines that identify it by some means, such as throwing sticks or coins. The lines of the hexagrams can be whole or broken, and each has a different combination.

The Moon appears through many of the hexagram chapters, and usually the phase is referred to as well: "The Moon's almost full…" In Chinese culture, the Moon seems to speak of female beauty and of female influences as well, such as love, marriage, and pregnancy. The full Moon is auspicious today in Chinese tradition, signifying brightness, peace, and reunion; in the I Ching, she may carry additional information based on the wording of the chapters. The chapters may be used as a meditative tool, as well as for divination.

NUMEROLOGY

Not entirely a method of divination, this is an ancient magical art that derives significance from ascertaining the numerological result of breaking down a name or other word. The letters of the alphabet are assigned a number in sequence, so that A = 1, B = 2, C = 3, up to the ninth letter, after which the sequence begins again at J = 1, then at S = 1.

From this table, a name can be given a numerological value in this way: let us take the name "John Smith" as an example:

J = 1, O = 6, H = 8, N = 5, S = 1, M = 4, I = 9, T = 2, H = 8. Adding up the letter values gives you 44. This is reduced again to give a single number: 4 + 4 = 8, which is your numerological result. This final number is then assessed for its planetary value, and each single number is associated with a planetary influence; for example, 1 = the Sun, 2 = the Moon, 3 = Mercury.

Witches and other magical practitioners use numerology for magic and make certain decisions based on it; for example, the choice of a magical name may be dictated by the birth number (arrived at by adding together the numerals of the birth date in the same way as we saw with the name). A witch may use their magical name strictly in circle, or they may use it publicly, including online, but it should tally with the witch's birth date.

The Moon rules number two and all things feminine, speaking of qualities like forgiveness, passiveness, domesticity, sensitivity, nurturing, and stability. She speaks of the need for balance and judgment and of partnerships and other dealings with others, whether positive or negative.

OGHAM

While the ancient Celts who used the Ogham alphabet for writing and divination used a lunar calendar, Robert Graves also based his "Tree Calendar" on the 28-day lunar cycle, giving each month a tree name. Some of these seem pretty inappropriate choices: rowan in January and February, when it is dormant, and holly—long associated with the winter solstice because of the glory of its red berries—in July, and he has also missed out important Ogham trees like apple, yew and blackthorn.

The Ogham that corresponds to the Tarot Moon card is Saille, Willow, which, like the rune Laguz, represents dreams, intuition and magic. The willow tree has always been associated with the Moon, because of its close relationship with water, its white wood, its silvery-coloured bark and the crescent shapes of its long pale leaves. It is associated with several Moon Goddesses, including Artemis/Diana, Hecate and Selene.

PALMISTRY

The Moon appears in palmistry as the Mount of Luna, which is the bottom "corner" of your palm next to the outside of your wrist, on the same side of the palm as your pinkie or smallest finger. The qualities of this part of the palm represent your imagination, intuition, and psychic powers, and also reveals an individual's empathy, compassion, and imagination. A palm reader will take note of the size of the mount, whether it is flatter or more protuberant, whether moist or dry, smooth or rough, and what lines lie across it to ascertain the extent of its influence over you.

RUNES

The rune symbols are not generally representational, although they may have started out as crude outlines of actual animals or other items. They are also composed entirely of straight lines, for ease of cutting them into wood and stones, so including a circular and curved shape like the Moon would be problematical.

The obvious rune to represent the Moon as an influence is Laguz, the rune of water, dreams, intuition and spiritual journeys. Laguz, the equivalent of our letter L, may represent a leek or maybe the head of a water monster, but it speaks of mysteries and even the occult. Goddesses were not that important in Norse belief, and the Moon was seen as a male deity.

SCRYING

Scrying can be done with a large number of media, such as clouds, inky water, smoke, mirrors, crystals or even your cosy winter fire. With the mind in a placid receptive state, the reader gazes into the medium, without trying to see anything in particular, and allows shapes and visions to form and give their meaning. For the meanings of Moon shapes in scrying, see Tasseomancy below.

THE TAROT

The first instance which springs to mind is the classic Tarot pack, which not only includes a card called *The Moon*, but in some packs has her make a guest appearance on several other cards as well. Tarot readers may also do special readings for themselves and for clients at certain phases of the Moon; at the new, for example, at the beginning of a new project, relationship or other life event; and at the full to help the subject to assess how well they have achieved their goals since their beginning; and during the waning Moon for advice on clearing away problems and maybe ending a bad relationship or leaving an unsatisfying job.

The oldest available Tarot pack around today is the "Marseilles" pack, which hails from Italy originally, probably during the Renaissance. Its images are fairly crude and simple, and the Moon appears only on the card named for her. However, the best-known example of the Tarot cards in use today is the pack previously known as the *Rider-Waite*, but now almost universally known as *Pamela Colman Smith's Tarot*, as she personally created the artwork on commission in the 1900s. The artwork on these is lush and detailed, and the Moon appears on several cards.

XVIII The Moon

The Moon frowns down, a crescent shape within the outline of the full, on a landscape in front of and beyond two castles or pylons, which includes a long road running away towards the horizon. In the foreground a crayfish or lobster attempts to climb out of the water, and two dogs, or a dog and a wolf, are howling at the Moon. There are small tear-shaped objects in the sky above them, perhaps a portrayal of the Moon's rays or night dews. This card is usually interpreted as indicating change and choices based on intuition and dreams or buried fears and speaks of female power.

II The High Priestess

The figure depicted in this card is inspired by the Goddess Isis, who sits between two very Egyptian-looking, lotus-topped columns and has a large crescent Moon lying at her feet. As she speaks of occult wisdom, secrets, spiritual journeys, and dreams, the Moon's presence here speaks for itself.

X The Wheel of Fortune

The wheel, marked with Hebrew letters and alchemical symbols, does not appear at first glance to reference the Moon or include it as a symbol. But it is a wheel, and it moves in a constant cycle of change, so I have always seen it as a lunar card. It turns in the sky between four chimerae (mythical beasts composed of more than one animal), representing the four elements or humours. On the wheel itself, a Sphinx sits at the top holding a sword and representing triumph. Yet its triumph is transitory, for other creatures on the wheel, a serpent and the mythological figure Hermanubis, will rise to the top in turn, and the Sphinx will fall, for the wheel represents fickle and ever-changing fortune.

The Two of Swords

A crescent Moon shines down on a figure—it is not possible to say whether it is a man or a woman—clad in a long white robe and seated on a bench beside the sea. The person is blindfolded and holds two long swords skywards in its crossed hands. This is a card of indecision, or even impasse, with the figure not able to see his or her way through their current problems. The Moon has her points facing downwards, perhaps as a small point of hope in the card's imagery.

The Eight of Cups

In this card, eight golden cups are stacked in the foreground, three on top of five. Behind them, the man who arranged them is walking away, perhaps to fetch wine to fill them, or perhaps he is just leaving them because they cannot give him what he wants. Above the scene, the Moon shines down, both as a waning sliver and a full Moon, which indicates the end of something. Perhaps the man has put his all into a situation—a relationship, a career, a project—and now knows he cannot prevail, so is abandoning it.

The King of Swords

This card speaks of a benevolent authority figure, ruling with intelligence and compassion. The *Smith* deck shows him with a canopy above his head that includes butterflies and crescent moons—both symbols of transformation.

There are many different Tarot packs, and I do not have the time nor the space to go into them all here, but a look at a very similar pack will show you that others also have something extra to offer if you are seeking one particular image. The beautiful American *Morgan-Greer* pack, loosely based on Colman Smith's symbology but owing more to vibrant colour, chosen for astrological reasons, and to simplicity than to detail, also has the Moon pictured in *The Hierophant* and *The Chariot*. The hierophant wears a crescent Moon as a gorget; this, like *The High Priestess*, speaks of your spiritual journey; the crescent makes sense as a symbol of renewed hope and guidance. *The Chariot*, the card of progression, shows the charioteer wearing crescent moons as earrings or epaulettes. As they are mirror images, one is crescent, the other waning, which gives another layer of meaning to this card about conflict.

TASSEOMANCY (TEA LEAF READING)

Tasseomancy, sometimes called tasseography, is done by enjoying a nice cup of tea (made from loose-leaf tea instead of a teabag) and then examining the patterns in the leaves left behind. It is surprising what shapes you can see in such an apparently unpromising medium. A clever friend of mine who is writing a book on the subject gave me a few ideas about this.

Some of the meanings of a Moon shape are as you would expect: a waxing crescent speaks of new beginnings and an auspicious time for beginning new projects, while a waning Moon shape (with the horns to the right as you look at her) warns that the querent should be wary of travelling over water and should ideally refrain from any new undertakings. Generally speaking, the Moon appearing in a reading speaks of the rhythms of time, of the querent being conscious of these and of behaving generally in a punctual way. However, other factors have to be taken into consideration, such as where the shape appears in the cup and what other shapes are nearby... As with most divination, it is not as simple as it appears and may require an experienced reader to explain the full picture.

WITCH'S RUNES

These are "tellstones" of a similar kind to runes, yet far less well-known, and their origins seem lost in the mists of time. The sets may vary from 8 to 13 symbols, which always include the Sun and Moon.

Depending on the medium and the person who created them, these stones may have a fairly basic image on them, or an artistic and colourful one. The Moon may be a simple crescent outline or a silver symbol embellished with tiny stars and wavy lines. It represents the psychic and feminine influence of the Moon and can also represent a female person in the question (in sets that do not include the "man" and "woman" symbols) or the period of a month when the question includes a time element. If a "yes or no" question is asked, the Moon signifies no.

But it is also the Goddess's own symbol and speaks of cycles, tides, birth, inspiration, magic, mystery, dreams and visions, inspiration, beauty, and the occult. It also covers travel, hotels, property, and the food industry, for some reason. It could be indicating your spiritual path, and it strongly indicates your past, your family background, and issues arising from your childhood. Madness may be in the equation too—it is something associated with the Moon and her powers. This could be the madness of obsessive love. The Moon is not necessarily a positive witch's rune, and she may indicate betrayal, secrets, and lies.

THE QABALAH

The Qabalah is a system of thought derived from Jewish mysticism, a kind of map of the spiritual universe, with ten spheres—plus one concealed one—called *sephiroth* placed at intervals on a symbolic tree that also has 22 paths joining all its points. The Qabalah has become extremely influential in Hermetic and Thelemic belief, also Masonry, and has been used in magic and spiritual practice. Qabalists also connect the 22 paths to the 22 Major Arcana Tarot cards, as well as to the letters of the Hebrew alphabet that identify the paths, while the cards of the Minor Arcana are also linked to the sephiroth.

The sephiroth are said to represent the qualities of God, while the paths describe ways of achieving a greater closeness to God, or they may represent the higher human qualities and the ways of achieving them to grow closer to the Divinity.

The sephirah (this is the singular form of sephiroth) linked to the Moon is Yesod, which forms a sort of gateway to the upper sephiroth, as it is positioned above Malkuth (the Earth) and is said to reflect light down from the upper spheres onto the Earth. Yesod is masculine but represents some qualities we have come to see as feminine, such as dreams and intuition, empathy and compassion, and the element of water. The path linked to the Tarot Moon card is 29 Qoph, which stretches from Malkuth, the lowest sephirah representing the Earth, to Netzach, the lowest in the right-hand column, without touching Yesod. Qoph is known as *physical intelligence and* is linked to Pisces and the back of the head. Confusingly, Qoph, the equivalent of our letter K, is the 19th letter of the Hebrew alphabet, yet as a Qabalah path, it is number 29.

Pathworkings and meditations on the paths are a recognized way of using the Qabalah, whether for divination, magic, or spiritual development.

CHAPTER NINE

The Magic of the Moon

"What other body could pull an entire ocean from shore to shore? The Moon is faithful to its nature and its power is never diminished."
— Deng Ming Dao, Chinese philosopher and artist

One thing everyone knows about witches is that they gather by moonlight on a spooky deserted moor, probably with a huge simmering cauldron in the middle overflowing with frogs' toes and newts' eyes, naturally all wearing pointy hats and carrying broomsticks (the witches that is, not the amphibians), with their black cats and other familiars at their sides, to perform magic to curse a neighbour or cause a ship to be dashed on the rocks. Oh, and they invoke the Devil. I'll give you two out of ten for this little bit of nonsense because we do love moonlight, and we do perform magic. And very often these two things go hand-in-hand, for the simple reason that we regard the Moon as a giant powerhouse for our work. Wherever magic comes from—and opinions vary—most witches would agree that it works better if there is a full or new Moon in the equation. However, this is not a hard and fast rule, as the Moon in all her manifestations works for some kind of magic.

For starters, the full Moon herself is never "just" a full Moon, for astrologically-minded magical practitioners take into account the zodiac sign in which she is being full or new and may even also note the planets that are making aspects to it. Then, in addition to the 12 or 13 lunations in a year, pagans also observe the less regular occurrences.

SUPERMOON

A supermoon can be either new or full and occurs when the Moon comes to the closest point near the Earth in her orbit, known as the perigee. There are generally three or four supermoons in a year.

BLUE MOON

A full lunation takes 29.5 days, and there are 365 days in a year, leaving 11 days over; therefore, there will in some years be more than 12 full Moons. The second full Moon in a calendar month is called the Blue Moon, and it can have magical meaning and power beyond an ordinary full Moon (in some circumstances the Moon may actually appear bluish, but that is generally down to some kind of pollution such as wildfires or volcanic activity). Magical practitioners may keep this event for special magics, utilizing what they see as an extra heavy-duty battery for their work.

The Blue Moon can also be defined as the third full Moon in a season containing four (summer and winter). It is confusing, as news stories across the internet can refer to either definition.

BLACK MOON

Because of the discrepancy between the length of 12 lunations and the solar year, there will also at some stage be more than

12 dark Moons in a year. The second dark in a calendar month is called the Black Moon, and it can have magical meaning and power beyond an ordinary dark Moon. Generally, the energies of the normal dark or waning Moon are seen as magnified at this time, in the same way as the Blue Moon—an entirely manmade concept, if you think about it, yet not without merit.

The Black Moon can also be defined in the same way as a Blue Moon, as the third dark Moon in a season containing four, but also as the *absence* of a new Moon or full Moon in February, in which, as a 28-day month, this is a rare possibility.

BLOOD MOON/ECLIPSE

The Blood Moon is a term given to the Moon when she is in total eclipse; usually she can still be seen through the Earth's shadow as a dim blood-red sphere. A lunar eclipse happens only when the Earth is directly between the Sun and the Moon, up to five times a year, though usually only two. Around one-third of these are total eclipses.

The energies of the total eclipse are seen as a magnified version of the ordinary full and are used for charging and cleansing special items. Crystals, tools, Tarot cards, and runes can be left out during the eclipse to be cleansed of negative energies—perhaps from someone else having handled them—while a dish of water or oil can also be set out to charge with eclipse power for use on a later occasion. As with the full Moon—see below—the eclipse energies can be used for setting intentions.

ASTROLOGICAL MOON MAGIC

Most properly trained witches feel it is important to try to use a time when the Moon is in an astrological sign that is appropriate for the nature of their working. Remember that each astrological sign is ruled by a planet, and in witchcraft the planets all have their own sphere of influence. Each sign is also assigned to one of the elements, so there is another layer of influence. They may also take into account the Sun's current zodiac sign and whether there are any aspects common to both the Sun and Moon (obviously, at the full Moon, the Sun and Moon are always in opposition—that is, at opposite sides of the Earth).

The "personality" of each sign will influence the Moon or Sun, and thus the magical power. A fairly basic primer on astrology will tell you about each sign—and whether or not you scoff at the idea, you will find that friends and family seem to conform to their astrological sign more often than not. So, a Libran will be a peacemaker keen to step in when two friends are quarrelling, and a Piscean will be a dreamer of dreams, while it has been my experience that people who practise magic have a strong Aquarian or Uranian influence somewhere in their birth chart.

Moon Sign	Planetary Ruler	Element	Key Words
Aries	Mars	Fire	Action/enthusiasm
Taurus	Venus	Earth	Renewal/sensuality
Gemini	Mercury	Air	Communication/knowledge
Cancer	The Moon	Water	Emotion/nurturing
Leo	The Sun	Fire	Vitality/determination
Virgo	Mercury	Earth	Organising/studiousness
Libra	Venus	Air	Balance/co-operation
Scorpio	Pluto	Water	Sexuality/philosophy
Sagittarius	Jupiter	Fire	Truth/justice
Capricorn	Saturn	Earth	Patience/groundedness
Aquarius	Uranus	Air	Innovation/sociability
Pisces	Neptune	Water	Sensitivity/idealism

THE MAGIC OF THE MOON

Moon in Aries is the best time to work magic involving leadership, authority, rebirth, spiritual conversion, or willpower. This might be surprising, as you might expect this of the sign of Leo, but Leo has its own correspondences which differ somewhat from strong, warlike Mars.

Moon in Taurus is the best time to work magic for love, property, material acquisitions, and money. As I have said, I have always felt that Taurus—ruled by the Love Goddess Venus—should be a cow, rather than an aggressive bull.

Moon in Gemini is the best time to work magic for good communication, change of residence, writing, public relations, and travel.

Moon in Cancer is the best time to work magic for home and domestic life. Here the Moon is in her own sign, so will be even more powerful for any use to which you put her.

Moon in Leo is the best time to work magic involving authority, power over others, courage, fertility, or childbirth, also artistic and creative matters.

Moon in Virgo is the best time to work magic involving employment, intellectual matters, health, and dietary concerns.

Moon in Libra is the best time to work magic involving artistic work, justice, court cases, partnerships and unions, mental stimulation, and karmic, spiritual, or emotional balance.

Moon in Scorpio is the best time to work magic involving sexual matters, power, psychic growth, secrets, and fundamental transformations.

Moon in Sagittarius is the best time to work magic for publications, legal matters, travel, and truth.

Moon in Capricorn is the best time to work magic for organization, ambition, recognition, career, and political matters.

Moon in Aquarius is the best time to work magic involving science, freedom, creative expression, problem-solving, extrasensory abilities, friendship, and the breaking of bad habits or unhealthy addictions.

Moon in Pisces is the best time to work magic involving dreamwork, clairvoyance, telepathy, music, and the creative arts.

Many lunar calendars and diaries—and there are many on the market designed primarily for witches and other magical practitioners—will also give *void-of-course* information. Void-of-course means that the Moon is making no aspects to any planet, which happens on a regular basis as the satellite moves through the sky, and usually lasts only a few hours, or a day or two at the most. It concludes when she moves into a position to make an aspect with another planet (all heavenly bodies are known as "planets" in astrology, even the Sun), perhaps by moving into opposition (full Moon) or conjunction (dark Moon) with the Sun. Generally speaking, magical practitioners avoid starting or doing any magical work when the Moon is void-of-course.

As we saw with lunar gardening, certain types of magic are recommended only for certain phases of the Moon.

ENERGIES OF THE FULL

The Moon is at her strongest power at the full and can be used for any type of magic except spells for banishing and decreasing a problem (however, witches use "black elastic" and get around this by using the full Moon to *increase* the positive side, so that, for example, a smoker trying to quit and needing to work the magic at the full might cast a spell to *increase* his willpower, rather than working to decrease the addiction).

The full Moon has good clearing energies and can also be used to cleanse and charge magical tools, crystals, and water for the altar or spellwork. Simply leaving the items outside or even (perhaps if you live in a top-storey flat) on a windowsill or hung outside the window on a securely tied string in the moonlight will do the trick. Allowing moonlight to fall on spellwork of any kind is generally considered one way of giving your magic some bang for its buck, and the light of the full is especially desirable. One notable use of the full Moon is for the setting of intentions, perhaps into a tool, a crystal, or a container of water. This can then be used in future magical work for this end.

Many witches use full Moon water, either in spellwork or in ritual, from the salt and water blessing done as part of casting a circle to initiations. This is easily made at the full Moon—though other phases can also be used for different magical purposes. A dish of water is simply left out under the moonlight to charge with full Moon energies. Sterling silver or crystal is a traditional material for the bowl used in this way, but a plain glass one will do the job just as well. The water should be placed under the light of the full Moon, even if the Moon is hidden by cloud, as it will gather some of the energies, and of course not all nights are so cloudy that the Moon never appears at all. If you don't have a garden or other outside space, a windowsill can be used for this, but you might consider leaving the window open so the Moon's rays do not have to pass through the glass. I personally give the vessel some taps or blows as it stands in the silver light, and those familiar with the basics of homeopathy will recognize this as "succussion", which activates the ingredients in a manner not well understood. Hold the vessel so that it is filled with moonlight, then give it a couple of firm taps with your wand or some other wooden stick—a wooden kitchen spoon will do—being careful not to hit it hard enough to crack the container. The Moon water should be taken up in the very early morning, before the Sun's light has had a chance to touch it and add its own energies, and then stored in a dark place in a stoppered vessel.

If the *moment* of full falls at night (as it does roughly 50% of the time), you can take up the container and succuss it at that very instant, before taking it inside—as the Moon's energies "flip" at this point and become waning ones. Water that has received this level of attention can be used for more important spellwork and has greater energies than water that has been left out unattended overnight, so sometimes it is worth setting an alarm and getting out of bed to go and succuss the water and take it inside.

If you practise magic or ritual involving the Moon, making Moon water is a very useful habit to get into. Make it every month; you will be surprised how much you can use in a month of magic.

If you have watched any old werewolf movies, you will probably think the full Moon lasts for five days, but actually there is an *instant* of full, after which her energies immediately change to those of the waning Moon (if your eyesight is reasonable, you may well be able to see a slight difference between the actual full Moon and the outline of the Moon on the nights either side of the full). Most witches choose to meet and work in advance of this moment to take advantage of full Moon energies and avoid the "changeover", so that

Esbat, for example, may be held the day before the date of the full Moon if it falls at an inconvenient time for ritual, such as early morning or the middle of the day. You can think of it as a party balloon being blown up for a children's party by Dad, getting bigger and bigger, and more and more beautiful until suddenly ... bang! Dad has overdone it, and it pops.

So, what about the energies of the other phases? You can think of the Moon as being a pod on a giant Ferris wheel. It comes towards you, getting bigger and bigger as it approaches, then it arrives! It is time to get on and do that voodoo that you do so well. However, if you stay where you are, the wheel moves on, and the Moon sails away from you, getting smaller and smaller until she disappears altogether. These *departing* energies can be used, as can the disappearance, for other types of magic.

So, we will move on from the full Moon to the next phase.

ENERGIES OF THE WANING MOON

As the Moon moves on from the full, one side (the right, as you are looking at her) starts to be nibbled away by the shadow of the Earth. It is as though she is actually decreasing in size, and some cultures have told tales of sky monsters and dragons eating away at the Moon to explain this phenomenon.

This is the phase in which you can work negative magic—and I'm not talking about black magic, because I don't do that, and I strongly advise you not to either. This is the time when you can do any sort of reducing or banishing magic, from starting a diet or quitting smoking, with a bit of magical help, to a strong spell to cause your quarrelsome neighbour to leave you alone or your ex to stop posting smack about you online. Any kind of spell that involves limiting or banishing: binding spells, spells to give up bad habits, spells to stop evildoers from harming others, or spells to reduce harmful effects. The waning Moon is a good time for connecting with the Crone, and so a good time for psychic work, divination, pathworkings, and dreamwork.

Waning Moon magic can also be "tweaked" in the same way as with the full Moon. Perhaps you need to do a spell to increase your finances, but it is the time of the waning Moon. Change the tone of the spell to *decrease* your expenses this month, so you can meet your commitments.

ENERGIES OF THE DARK MOON

At this point, the Moon has disappeared from the sky. She may be above your head in a cloudless firmament, but you cannot see her because she has been blacked out by the Earth's shadow. Some people regard the dark and new as the same thing, but you must remember that, as with the full, there is an instant of new Moon, and the energies change at that instant. If you are working magic up to that instant, it should be a different kind than what you might do after the moment of the new Moon. Dark Moon is a time for meditation, for planning, and for prayer.

ENERGIES OF THE NEW MOON

After the full Moon, the new Moon is the next most powerful time for magic.

Whenever possible, follow nature's natural energy currents. There is a natural time for starting things (a planting time), for maturing things (a growing time), for reaping things (a harvest time), and, of course, a time for rest and planning (*to everything—turn, turn, turn—there is a season—turn, turn,*

turn ... take it away, Byrds!). Flowing with these currents will make your magical work much easier.

The Moon has moved away on the invisible Ferris wheel and has now reappeared on the other side and is coming towards you again. However, she performs in the opposite way to the full: the energies of the new Moon appear on the instant of new, and they stay as the Moon waxes. New Moon magic can be performed for three or four days after the instant of new. Probably, when you first see that tiny sliver of silver in the western sky, the main force of the new Moon energies has passed.

ENERGIES OF THE WAXING MOON

From the moment of the new Moon, the Moon is waxing, that is, growing, and she has the characteristic backwards-C crescent shape until she achieves half-Moon, then gibbous (more than half) as she approaches the full.

A waxing Moon is a good time for many of the spells and work you might do under the full, including spells for growth, fertility, love, spiritual development, and healing. It is also used for spells to draw things towards you, into your life. This aspect of the Moon can be seen as the deosil aspect in the circle (pagans use a sunwise, or clockwise, movement in the circle if they are doing positive magic; and a widdershins, or anti-clockwise, movement for banishing or decreasing magic). The waning or decreasing Moon is related to a widdershins movement.

The Names of the Moon

Influenced by Native American spirituality, modern pagans have given each full Moon a picturesque name. Whilst you may not agree with each one, it is useful in that the name sets the "flavour" of that month and its importance in the spiritual calendar. However, we may feel some of these Moon names have been applied to the wrong month—surely, for example, it is more natural to call March the Hare Moon, as we associate mad March hares with the month and with Ostara, the Spring Equinox, which falls in March. And surely October seems a little early in the year to expect snow.

January – Storm Moon

This cheerless month is the time of the year when the worst of winter's storms takes place, and people huddle inside their homes with the central heating whacked up high and curtains drawn against the wild nights. It is a time to appreciate the warmth and contentment of the hearth, but there is very little that is going on outside! It is also a time—like much of the winter—to explore yourself and plan the changes you will make in the spring.

February – Chaste Moon

This antiquated word for pure reflects the custom of greeting the New Year with a clear soul. The worst of winter has passed; here nature appears dead, grey, lifeless, and beaten. Yet this is an illusion; beneath the ground, new life lies buried, waiting to burst forth. Even in the worst and coldest weather, snowdrops will be bursting forth, perhaps other spring flowers too. Just as nature is awaiting the warmth of the Sun to return, ready to green the earth, so now is a time to put into action things conceived during winter. Pagans celebrate Imbolc, the herald of spring, and lunar Imbolc in February.

March – Seed Moon

Sowing season and symbol of the start of the agricultural year. The seasons are fickle, one moment warm, the next cold, but nature is slowly transforming, renewing itself. The Spring Equinox occurs during this month.

Winter is fading, and the hopes for the future months grow expectantly. New shoots can be seen; the first of spring's flowers show themselves. The tingle of life is growing; all is growing anew. With all this feverish activity, now is an excellent time for spring cleaning, for getting out and experiencing this zest for life.

April – Hare Moon

The sacred animal was associated in Roman legends with springtime and fertility. The days are growing longer; sunny, warm days provide a welcome relief from the previous month's cold and harshness. All of nature is constantly growing; each day holds new surprises. On each tree and flower, insects are starting to appear, hidden away in hibernation during the long months of winter, and already some plants have seeded, spreading next year's life to the winds. It is a good time for planning ahead: things planted now will bear fruit in the months ahead. Pagans also celebrate Beltane, the marriage of the God and Goddess, at the end of April and beginning of May.

May – Dyad Moon

The Latin word for a twin refers to the twin stars of the constellation of Castor and Pollux. Gemini, the sign of the Twins, runs from around 21st May into mid-June. The great energy that drives the spring growth is in full flow, and the hedgerows and woodlands are green with new life. Birds are nesting, and animals are caring for their young. The trees are decked in blossom for the wedding of the Goddess and God. It is time to look forward to the pleasures of the coming summer and care for young crops.

June – Mead Moon

This has nothing to do with the wine made from honey, beloved of pagans for ritual and celebration: June is a little early for collecting honey. During late June and most of July, the meadows, or meads, were mowed for hay. The summer reaches a peak at the Summer Solstice, the shortest night and longest day, and the weather grows warmer. Planting is still going on, but crops planted now will still bear fruit.

July – Wort Moon

When the Sun was in Leo, the worts (from the Anglo-Saxon *wyrt* = plant) were gathered to be dried and stored. The summer has passed its apogee, and the nights begin to grow longer, yet there is more sunshine and heat, and plants are still maturing. Nights are hot, and trees are in full leaf, yet some plants are already starting to go over, and the young animals and birds are growing to full maturity.

August – Barley Moon

This is the month of harvest, when the fields are golden and the corn is being cut. Farmers are often at work all through the night to bring in the golden hoard of grain before the weather can change. Sometimes this is a dry and dusty month, but there are fruits on the trees and nuts in the hedgerows, and everything feels filled to overflowing with goodness. Pagans celebrate Lughnasadh, or Lammas, the first harvest festival, in early August.

September – Blood Moon

This Moon and its name mark the season when domestic animals were sacrificed for winter provisions or because there was not enough feed for all of them to live on through the winter. Libra's full Moon occasionally became the Wine Moon when a grape harvest was expected to produce a superior vintage. The harvest continues, with fruits from the trees and hedgerow glowing like jewels and ready to pick. The leaves may have just started to turn, and colourful fungus may have started to grow in the grass and woods. In the past, animals would be readied for slaughter, and wood would be stockpiled in anticipation of the coming winter. The Autumn Equinox occurs during this month and is celebrated as the second harvest.

October – Snow Moon

Scorpio heralds the dark season when the Sun is at its lowest and the first snows fly. It marks the end of summer; nature has slowed down, the last of the harvests has been brought in, and the first hints of winter are showing. The trees, once crowned in colourful leaves, start to shed their golden canopy. Nature's final explosion of activity happens as plants and trees spread their seeds. It is a time for looking back at the year gone by, for putting things no longer needed behind you, and for preparing for the coming year. A time for finishing projects, cleaning out the debris of the past year, whether emotional or physical, and contemplating the personal targets and goals you have achieved. Samhain (Halloween) is celebrated at the end of October, as the time to honour the dead and as the third harvest.

November – Oak Moon

The sacred tree of the Druids and the Roman God Jupiter is most noble as it withstands winter storms. The beginning of winter is here, when days grow shorter and the nights longer. The time when the hints of winter to come are showing, chill winds blow, and frost forms, while the pale golden Sun's presence wanes. Nature is in regression; the summer visitors have left, squirrels have gathered their winter stores, and the first of winter's visitors are arriving. It is a time of inner reflection and growth, for divination and developing psychic talents.

December – Wolf Moon

The fearsome nocturnal animal represents the "night" of the year. This is the time of the long nights of winter, for until the Winter Solstice, the hours of daylight grow shorter. It is also a time of celebration at Yule, one of the cheery winter festivals of old. Unlike the Summer Solstice, Yule is a time of quiet celebration of the home and hearth and of friends and families. Although winter is upon us, the evergreen of holly symbolizes rebirth and new beginnings. It is a good time to start new projects.

PLANETARY HOURS

Carrying on the idea of magical timings for the best results, a system called *planetary hours* is known and used by some magical practitioners. When I started out on my path, planetary hours were recommended as the way to choose the right time for a spell. This involved knowing the exact time of sunrise and sunset and then referring to a timetable of hours that went like this:

Monday	*Tuesday*	*Wednesday*	*Thursday*	*Friday*	*Saturday*	*Sunday*
Moon	Mars	Mercury	Jupiter	Venus	Saturn	Sun
Saturn	Sun	Moon	Mars	Mercury	Jupiter	Venus
Jupiter	Venus	Saturn	Sun	Moon	Mars	Mercury
Mars	Mercury	Jupiter	Venus	Saturn	Sun	Moon
Sun	Moon	Mars	Mercury	Jupiter	Venus	Saturn
Venus	Saturn	Sun	Moon	Mars	Mercury	Jupiter
Mercury	Jupiter	Venus	Saturn	Sun	Moon	Mars
Moon	Mars	Mercury	Jupiter	Venus	Saturn	Sun
Saturn	Sun	Moon	Mars	Mercury	Jupiter	Venus
Jupiter	Venus	Saturn	Sun	Moon	Mars	Mercury
Mars	Mercury	Jupiter	Venus	Saturn	Sun	Moon
Sun	Moon	Mars	Mercury	Jupiter	Venus	Saturn

This system is based on the Chaldean order of planets, and each day or night is divided up into 12 "hours", with the day beginning at sunrise and ending at sunset—so some hours are going to be pretty short, as little as 35 minutes in daytime in the winter, while others will be much longer, up to an hour and 25 minutes in the summer. Simply measure the time between sunrise and sunset on the chosen day and divide this by 12; then you will be able to calculate when your correct hour falls. The table also continues on into night, which also divides into 12 in the same way. Note that the first hour of each day is dedicated to the planet of that day.

This is incredibly tedious to work out, and often the appropriate hour falls at a very difficult time to perform magic, like three in the morning or lunchtime (when you are at work). As a more experienced practitioner, I never now use this system, preferring to go by Moon phase and other factors.

OTHER FACTORS AND TIMINGS

The concept known as *correspondences* is a vast body of information taking in colours, perfumes, plants, animals, crystals, metals, times, dates, foods, and drinks, and cataloguing them all by planetary influence to make it easier to find the correct items to use in magic. So, for a love spell, you might use a pink cloth and a pink candle (pink being one of the colours associated with Venus, the planet of the Love Goddess), roses (preferably pink ones), rose incense, and, if you have one, a copper candle holder. All these things are listed under the correspondences of Venus—and fairly good lists of correspondences can be found in magical books or online. However, as well as doing the actual spell-working at the correct time, you can go a bit further with some of the ingredients, taking care to pick the roses, for example, in the *hour of Venus,* whether that falls in the day or night, or picking them under a full Moon that falls in Taurus or Libra—both Venus signs.

The Moon, of course, has its own set of correspondences, which are suitable for Moon magic, including magic involving cycles and tides, inspiration of all kinds, women's matters and childbirth, travel, and psychic work.

These include, and this is a far from complete list:

Day of the week: Monday.

Colours: because the Moon has three different aspects, she is associated with (new) silver, white or pale grey, (full) red, and (waning) black.

Metal: silver.

Gems: moonstone, pearl and mother-of-pearl, rock crystal, quartz, abalone and other shell-based gems, aquamarine, opal, selenite.

Plant materials, including essential oils: aloe, bananas, birch, cabbage, camphor, chamomile, chickweed, coconut, cucumber, eucalyptus, frangipane, ginseng, grapes, honesty, jasmine, lemon and lemon balm, lily, lotus, mallow, moonflower (white morning glory), moonwort, motherwort, myrtle, orris root, poppy, potatoes, pumpkin, purslane, rose (white), sandalwood, turnips, seaweed, vervain, water lily, wintergreen, and also leafy vegetables, especially lettuce.

Tree: willow trees.

Animals: hares and rabbits, cats, elephants, moths, shellfish, bats, snails, frogs, geese, and swans.

Tarot: the Moon and the High Priestess.

Astrology: the sign of Cancer.

Qabalah: Yesod.

Ogham: Saille (willow).

Element: water.

Number: three.

CHAPTER TEN

The Protection of the Moon

"The Moon does not fight. It attacks no one. It does not worry. It does not try to crush others. It keeps to its course, but by its very nature, it gently influences."
– Deng Ming-Dao, Chinese philosopher

Any witch or other occultist will tell you that there are astral entities that can attach themselves to you—or your home—and become quite unpleasant, especially if you practise magic or open yourself spiritually in any way. Anyone working with so-called supernatural forces is likely to be in the position of at least starting to open their chakras (see below) as they begin to develop. Open chakras are like open doors; just as they allow the psychic powers of their owner to expand and develop, they can also allow unwanted guests to stroll in and make themselves at home. Your home may also be at risk from what I like to call "beasties" if you practise occult rites in there without the proper procedures, and also if the home has been the setting for any unfortunate circumstances, such as violent crime, deep unhappiness, or sudden death, or if it has unusual underlying qualities such as a black (negative) ley line, subterranean water, or is built on a site that is sensitive in some way, such as having been a burial site or sacred site, or if it has a portal to other worlds (this is very rare, so don't go imagining that all sorts of *Poltergeist* horrors are likely to invade your home!).

A further danger—which you may feel is too strong a word for this, but I would not agree—is from vampires. And I am not talking about the sort of red-eyed, befanged creatures who turn up in horror films, but real people who have an unfortunate *gift*. We've all known these needy sorts of people who always seem to have a major crisis brewing in their lives, right? What happens is that some never have learned how to maintain their own energy or draw upon natural energies to keep themselves whole and in good condition spiritually as they should. These people continually seek out others that will allow themselves to be attached to. Have you ever come to dread seeing a neighbour or acquaintance because when you spend time talking with them, you feel depressed and exhausted afterwards? This sort of person will make it difficult for you to draw away; they will "need your support," "value your friendship," want to see you, phone you, and call round, never getting the message that you don't enjoy their company. Commonly they have poor physical health, which they dearly love to talk about! The result is that your energy levels drop substantially, and chaos can and will begin to occur in your life, as well as the potential for growing health problems. Essentially, these people, while we can and do have sympathy and concern for them, are psychic vampires, and we need to protect ourselves. Once we learn to do this, they lose interest in us, because they can no longer draw on our energies, and they drift away—or you can still spend time with these people and care for their well-being, even choose to let them have a little of your energy to let them feel better, and then close off the flow.

There are also people, who should know better, who deliberately use magic to prey upon others in the same way.

People who do not practise witchcraft or occultism may also encounter beasties (though they may not recognize that this is the problem) in other ways. These can include living in a psychically compromised home, playing with Ouija boards, and taking psychedelic drugs. Many years ago I had a friend who practised as a qualified psychotherapist, specializing in hypnotherapy and regression therapy for issues such as smoking and weight. He told me he could always tell when a patient had taken LSD in the past because they almost always had something "attached" to them, a dark beastie, which he was then able to detach and send away. In the situation where someone is living in a haunted house, that can be helped by the right rituals performed by someone who knows what they are doing, though it is not unknown for the beasties to return later on, as time in our world is not the same as time in theirs. As for Ouija boards, the simple rule for the inexperienced, which I cannot overemphasize, is *do not touch them with a ten-foot white-painted pole with a rubber glove on the end!* In psychic terms, it is like walking naked through a police no-go neighbourhood wearing all your jewellery at once and singing, "Poor Little Rich Girl," at the top of your voice.

Wiccan teachings are a very good path to follow, in that they lay down simple but effective procedures for practising witchcraft, divination, or other magical practises in a safe way and for protecting oneself from dangers and nuisances along the way. If you use these procedures carefully and mindfully, they will do what it says on the tin.

Bringing the Moon into protective practices is something many witches already do, partly because the Moon is deeply associated with their Goddess, partly because this amazing satellite of ours gives her power so readily to anyone with the knowledge to use it.

THE PROTECTION OF THE MOON

Moon amulets can be created in almost any medium, though obviously sterling silver is the optimum choice, with lunar protective sigils and symbols. Mother-of-pearl or some other shell is a good choice, as these natural shapes are white or whitish and are quite easy to whittle down to create a crescent shape. The finished amulet can then be charged and activated under full moonlight. The horseshoe has long been seen as magical and protective due to its iron constitution and its association with blacksmiths—still seen by some as semi-wizards handling a miraculous substance. It is generally seen as lucky whether worn as a piece of jewellery, on a bride's ensemble, or attached to a house or business, and is associated in some people's minds with the Moon, perhaps because of its rough crescent shape and its association with lunar Goddesses such as Rhiannon and Selene. The Romans held the crescent shape to be magically effective because of its double association with the Goddess Diana. Not only was she a Moon Goddess, but the crescent resembled the hunting horn she carried as Goddess of the Hunt.

Today a huge range of protective Moon amulets can be found in magic shops and online, many including protective crystals such as black tourmaline and obsidian. The Turkish amulet known as the Nazar Boncuk (it looks like a little eye made from blue and white glass) and the Hand of Fatima, or Hamsa, a North African charm that looks like a hand with two thumbs, are also commonly adorned with crescent moons that are believed to amplify their protective powers.

This being the golden age of subcutaneous inks, many witches and others have had themselves tattooed with protective symbols, including often quite complex designs incorporating the Moon and her phases, interwoven with sigils. These can be applied to any part of the body, but experienced practitioners may opt to place tattoos on psychically important points, such as over chakras. Some priestesses I know belonging to a Cornish Order have had crescent Moon tattoos done on their foreheads, just below the hairline, in a very light shade, so that it is almost invisible and would certainly go unnoticed by those not in the know. But the wearer knows it is there and benefits from its protective and spiritual presence.

Many magical practitioners use small, personalized rituals to protect themselves in all sorts of situations, from aggressive people on the streets to dark entities they encounter on the astral. These can be as simple as imagining a star of blue light on the brow to a full-scale suit of shining white armour. Here below are two examples.

EXERCISE ONE

This useful little ritual involves sitting or standing with one's feet planted flat on the ground. Take three or four deep, relaxing breaths, or practise square breathing[2] for a few moments.

Now, close your eyes, and in your mind look down through the ground beneath you, through the layers of soil and rocks and other layers, until you reach the Earth's core. Now draw up the Earth's energies through the layers, through the ground, through one's feet and into one's body. These can be visualised as strings or ribbons of coloured light, green or red or gold. When they have reached the heart, you can then

---

2 Square breathing involves taking in a long breath to the count of, say, three. The breath is then held, again to the count of three, and released to the count of three. The empty lungs are then held for another three, before beginning the cycle over again. Depending on your lung capacity and your familiarity with this procedure, the holding count can be increased to four or five or even six.

send your personal energies up into the sky in search of the Moon, and use them to pull down protective energies from there, in the form of silver or white strings. These are then mixed within the body, to create an astral glow of power and protection. Many practitioners have their own version of this rite, for which the only requirement needed is a little privacy and the only equipment the ability to visualise.

EXERCISE TWO

This can be performed under the full Moon, or the Moon can be visualized. Obviously, the best scenario is to perform it, at least for the first time, under the real Moon, but this is not always possible in our cloudy country—or within the constraints of our modern lives. However, the night before I wrote this was a full Moon, and I went outside—as I always do—to perform certain rites. The Moon was completely covered in thick cloud, and yet the night was bright (I am fortunate enough to live in an area with almost no light pollution). Some does get through!

Stand under the Moon, real or imagined, and perform the breathing routines in the last exercise to still and ground yourself.

For this exercise, keep your eyes open if you are standing in moonlight, but close them if you are *visualizing* the Moon.

In your mind, feel the silvery light falling on your head and shoulders, so that it eventually builds to a penumbra of light in the shape of an umbrella. Slowly build this shape until it grows into a globe, completely surrounding you in protective light. Feel this light become firm and impenetrable. You can also fashion the light into a hooded cape, visualizing it covering you completely down to the floor, then *reach up* in your imagination and pull the hood down over your head and face, "concealing" yourself completely. With practice, this kind of visualization is easy to maintain and will protect you just as well as a cast circle.

With a little practice, you can carry this protective moonsuit with you wherever you go and summon it at a moment's notice if you feel threatened or afraid. Incidentally, these kinds of exercises are very beneficial when used just before you enter a supermarket, or other place filled with negative energies. Supermarkets can often be full of very unhappy people giving off negative vibes, because grocery shopping is boring and tiresome, and also perhaps because they are worried about the money they are spending—this vibe is noticeably worse in times of national financial depression.

CHAKRAS

We will meet these energy centres in later chapters, but here is a brief introduction to them, as they are also important in protection. Chakras are opened before beginning any spiritual work, but, in this chapter, we are looking at closing the chakras. It is quite a large subject, so I will confine myself to a few simple rules for closing down. It's a bit like going around making sure all the windows in your home are closed before you go away for the weekend. If you are familiar with the process of opening your chakras deliberately for magical work, you can simply reverse the process. As always, visualization is one of the most useful items in your toolbox.

Starting at the top, close down the crown chakra, but not completely: this one is a bit like a very top attic window, which you leave open a crack so bad smells don't build up. Then proceed on down the spine, closing all the others tightly. This is done by visualization: you can spin the chakras shut like coloured wheels or close them like real windows or draw down imaginary blinds, all colour-coded to fit with the correspondences of these centres ... Find a visualization that works for you.

The main seven centres are:

Sahasrara, the crown. Associated with the colour white or purple, it is located on the crown of the head.

Ajna, the "third eye". Associated with either indigo or purple, it is between and slightly above the eyebrows.

Vishuddha, the throat chakra, is situated near the voice box and associated with the colour blue.

Anahata, the heart, associated with the colour green.

Manipura, the solar plexus, which is associated with the colour yellow.

Svadhishthana, the sacral chakra, in the lower abdomen, is associated with the colour orange.

Muladhara, the base, is the bit you sit on, between the anus and the genitals, and is associated with the colour red.

PROTECTION OF THE HOME

A few years ago, we had some pretty fearful storms over Cornwall, where I live. Well, we have them most winters, actually, but at that time our roof was in a somewhat parlous state, and I was in constant fear that the next 60mph gust would strip the whole lot off and dump it on the drive, leaving us looking up into the sky. The roof has been rebuilt now, but at the time we were waiting for the work to be done, the weather seemed to be really trying to damage our humble home.

I went outside under the light of the full Moon and created and dropped a golden net over the roof. This only needed to be done once, after which I could simply reinforce it with visualization as I sat snugly indoors. The net was golden because that was the colour of the Moon I saw as I created the spell and the colour I felt drawn to using. Never at any stage after that did we lose more than a couple of tiles—even though when the builders did arrive to take off the old roof, they found it was held on by a few rusted nails, rotted battens, and willpower! This is an example of how the Moon will work for you if you build a relationship with her and believe it can be done (no magic can work if the practitioner themself does not believe in it!).

But, of course, she can also be helpful in protecting the inside of the house from nasties and beasties and things that go bump in the night. Your threshold itself holds an innate protective power that is as old as the very first caves and mud huts inhabited by our ancestors, but there is no harm in beefing up this protective power by any means you choose.

A Moon charm for your front door—or all your doors, if you have more than one—is very simply made and does not have to be conspicuous. A hanging basket by your door or in your porch can hide all sorts of things, as can larger, floor-standing plant pots. You can hide any amulets among the foliage or even bury them in the compost inside the pot.

A very ancient idea is the threshold amulet or deity. If you honour a protective Moon Goddess, it is easy to put a small image of her on the doorway and just ask her mentally as you go in or out to protect your home and those in it. The image can be placed where outsiders will not see it, perhaps up in the corner of the doorframe, or you can hide the image behind a piece of blank paper or card, or again, pop it into a hanging plant basket—such useful things!

THE PROTECTION OF THE MOON

Another magically important part of your home, which is appropriate for the placing of protective amulets, is the central "hearth" of your home, though nowadays, with not many houses being built with proper open fireplaces, this may be a cooker, a wood burner, or a central heating boiler rather than a real fireplace. If you are unsure, think of what you feel is the heart or centre of your home—the place you cook or might be likely to huddle if you felt cold. If you are fortunate enough to own an Aga or similar range, this will serve very well. Protective amulets can be placed on the hearth itself or hung on the chimney breast (perhaps behind a picture or other ornament if you are not 100% out of the broom closet). Moon energies can also be trapped in a spirit bottle: this is a pretty glass bottle (perhaps found in a charity shop or at the back of a cupboard you were clearing out), which is filled with crystals and pleasant herbs, before a protective spirit is invited to come and live in it. Use Moon crystals like selenite and moonstone in the jar, and leave it under full moonlight, as with the Moon water, and maybe include a silver crescent charm in the contents. Both the bottle and the house should be placed inconspicuously in or near the hearth. Remember to speak to the spirit in the house every day (even if it's just a muttered "good morning") and to dust his bottle regularly.

Some of these ideas can also be used in your car, starting with a Moon amulet hung from the rear-view mirror. Many people hang good luck symbols inside their cars anyway, or you can disguise it with an air freshener, and no muggle will think anything of it.

When my husband started his London-based job many years ago, he had to drive many miles, and I was always worried he would be in an accident. I lay on the pavement one morning and painted some protective symbols, including a crescent Moon and the symbol for Anubis (who is also a guide and protector, as well as being associated with the Moon) on the matt black underside of his bumper with shiny black enamel. He never knew it was there, but it seemed to work, and I certainly felt better for it!

CHAPTER ELEVEN

Lunar Healing

"The beautiful Moon is an antidepressant. Love for her light is in every heart because she is so friendly, loving and forgiving."

– Dr Debasish Mridha

It is the Sun that magical healers generally regard as being important in healing: it is part of the Sun's correspondences and its meanings in runes, scrying, and tarot. Despite what we now know about the harmful effects of baring our skin to its rays, people still think of sunshine as connected with health— and it is in many ways, including its role in the production of vitamin D by the body, as well as serotonin, its help in boosting the immune system, in neutralizing many harmful bacteria and viruses, and in producing a state of warmth and mental and physical well-being that encourages good health. The Moon reflects the Sun's light only in tiny amounts, yet she also can be powerfully useful in healing and healing magic ... who knew?

The nature of the Moon and her light goes some way to explaining this: the Moon and her light have an innate sense of calm about them, sailing in a dark and velvety sky. Peace and calm are basic requirements for healing (as against stress and anxiety, which can exacerbate and even set off all kinds of conditions), and moonlight delivers peace, calm, groundedness, and balance in barrowfulls. Meditating in moonlight is generally more successful, and deeper states of relaxation can be achieved, which can also benefit your health.

The beautiful Japanese therapy known as *shinrin-yoku*, which involves immersing one's being in the energies of nature, specifically in woods, is known to bring many benefits in the form of lowered stress levels, heart rate, and blood pressure and a more positive outlook. But many practitioners squeeze the very last bit of healing from this process by doing it under the full Moon, the theory being that the Moon's energies can only amplify the wise and kindly energies of the trees, the fresh air, and the peace of the surroundings. I would strongly agree that this makes sense—as long as you are careful and do not expose yourself to any danger at night in a dark place where strangers may pass through. I would also add that shinrin-yoku can be adapted for the other phases of the Moon, depending on what health or mental condition you hope to address. Tired, lethargic, and depressed? Try forest bathing (as shinrin-yoku is known) under the first visible crescent of the new Moon, or maybe the fuller waxing Moon if you need a zap of energy for an important project. If you are stressed out and maybe overweight, suffering from addictive conditions such as alcohol or tobacco dependency, try the waning Moon. At all times, keep in your mind the awareness of why you have chosen this phase and what you hope to achieve. In magic, we say, "intention is all," which is a bit simplistic but helpful overall. And this concept can be transferred to healing as well.

As I mentioned in Chapter Three, the Moon and her different phases certainly seem to impact human cycles. And as such, these phases are also useful as a timetable for self-care. You are probably getting the idea now, but just to clarify: use the new phase for new beginnings, the waxing Moon for growth, the full for extra boosts and achievement, and the waning phase for limitation, tailing off, and setting boundaries. This can be carried through all kinds of areas of your life, from diet and exercise to social interactions, career moves, and relationship changes.

The new Moon is an excellent time for kicking off a new regime: perhaps joining a gym or a walking club or starting a new kind of healthier or weight-reducing diet. Keep the diet robust at this phase, with plenty of protein, healthy, high- and low-glycaemic index carbohydrates, and fresh vegetables and fruit, and do not worry too much about weight gain: this phase gives a lot of energy, so you will be burning off more calories than at other phases. Eggs, fresh fish, lean meat, and salads are particularly beneficial at this time (when are they not?), and you may well feel drawn to eating these foods and to being more aware of your body's needs as the intuition encouraged by the new Moon puts you more closely in touch with your physical self. This is the time for that rock-climbing holiday or more physical activity generally, as well as an auspicious time for new starts, including new relationships, joining new groups and clubs, and taking up new activities and hobbies. You will find that you have enough energy for all of it!

The waxing phase will help you carry on your good intentions and give you the energy to do so, but at this phase you should start to watch your calorie intake and move away from carbs and more towards leaner meats, vegetables, leaves, and fruits. You don't want to be getting on the bathroom scales at the full and finding an unwanted gain. All the new ideas and beginnings you made at the new will go on developing and building in this phase as you build on your new starts. The first quarter (when the Moon is a semicircle with her round side to the right) flags up a good time for assessing what you have achieved and whether your regime needs adjusting.

At the full, you may well find you have an increased appetite and a tendency to retain fluid as well as genuine weight, but you may also have plenty of energy.... The full is a problematic time: some people find it suits them very well, and their health and energy levels may bloom; others find it stressful, with their sleep patterns affected and anxiety, emotional ups and downs, and nervous energy leading to exhaustion. Some regular meditation or other relaxation exercises will help with this. However, they may find themselves comfort-eating to compensate: many people do find that the full brings on cravings for things like chocolate and ice cream, but fortunately this effect is reasonably short-lived.

Then the waning Moon comes to the rescue, the cravings retreat, and the retained fluid should go away, hopefully taking some of the gained weight with it. Allow yourself to be less active, catch up on sleep, and rest generally; be gentle with yourself. If you want a night in with the telly, don't make yourself go out dancing. Energy levels may well be lower in this phase, but it should be easier to resist eating high-calorie foods packed with fat and sugar. Stick to a healthy diet with plenty of fibre and drink lots of water, as body systems—including the digestive system—can be sluggish at this time.

The benefits of following the Moon phases are manifold. They are easy to follow, for the information on the Moon is available everywhere from the internet to the sky above you, and the practice will encourage your body to align with an important natural rhythm, which will boost levels of well-being, relaxation, and energy. I often think that many of the ills that beset our twenty-first-century lifestyles have to do with our divorce from natural rhythms: we keep our eyes firmly on the clock, the television, our phone, and the computer screen, and never look up to see what the weather is doing, what the Moon is doing, or what season it is.

These Moon phases and their influences are reasonably straightforward for anyone to understand, but it can be taken further. If you have any knowledge of astrology, you may feel drawn to checking the zodiac sign in which your phase is occurring and the effects this sign could have on your regime. For example, at a full Moon in Sagittarius, you may feel that you should pay more attention to your diet and coddle your liver (ruled by Jupiter, which rules Sagittarius), perhaps giving yourself a break from alcohol and from rich, fatty foods, while at a new Moon in Virgo you may feel drawn to a strict fast or a colon cleanse. Of course, these effects may not last long, as the Moon only stays in one sign for a couple of days, so it makes sense to take advantage of them while they last.

For those who are interested in the zodiac signs and their effects and rulerships, below is a table showing the Moon signs that are appropriate for work on healing the different parts of the body.

Moon Sign	Planetary Ruler	Body Parts
Aries	Mars	Face, head or brain
Taurus	Venus	Throat, neck and ears
Gemini	Mercury	Shoulders, arms, hands and lungs
Cancer	The Moon	Chest and stomach
Leo	The Sun	Upper back, spine and heart
Virgo	Mercury	Intestines and nervous system
Libra	Venus	Lower back and kidneys
Scorpio	Pluto	Reproductive organs
Sagittarius	Jupiter	Liver, thighs and hips
Capricorn	Saturn	The bones and joints, teeth and skin
Aquarius	Uranus	Calves, ankles and blood
Pisces	Neptune	Feet and lymphatic system

Note that the Moon in the sign of Virgo is an excellent time to perform any kind of healing magic.

As with magic, the Moon's light can be used in a more direct way to effect healing for yourself and others. The healing properties of crystals and herbs can be amplified by the application of moonlight, and the light itself can be magnified with a little ingenuity and a couple of mirrors stood behind the container. Discoveries in recent years, including the research of the strangely well-named Masaru Emoto, have shown that energies, including emotions, can be captured in water, and while water itself has also been associated with healing, adding the energy of the Moon, as well as that of crystals and herbs, can really bring power to that healing. Bearing this in mind while you work on preparing potions and elixirs, you should ensure that you are careful to control your state of mind while handling the ingredients: a calm and positive witch will make for a soothing and healing potion; while, if you are distracted, in a bad mood, or just frantically busy and unable to give the process the time and care it needs, the potion will not be nearly so efficacious and may in fact do more harm than good. The easiest way to achieve this calm is to clear your mind and look directly into the face of the Moon, allowing her energies to infiltrate your entire being. Five or ten minutes of this lunar therapy should ensure you are in the right frame of mind to get on with the work at hand.

Healing potions, whether for internal consumption or anointing, benefit enormously from being stood in moonlight, adding the frequencies of the Moon's light to those of the stones and plants being used magically. Many herbal and crystal potions (not really at all like the fairy story idea of a bubbling cauldron filled with unsavoury animal parts and poisonous plants) can be brewed or steeped using non-poisonous ingredients—but check the properties of the plants first, as magical healing may not use the same plants as herbal simples, which act chemically in the same way as pharmaceuticals.

The very water for the potion can be Moon water, that is, water that has already been stood in the light of the full Moon

LUNAR HEALING

(see Chapter Nine). It is always better to use natural water for this, perhaps from rainwater, or a nearby stream, or even, if you are lucky enough to have one on your property—and many older houses, particularly rural ones, do—from your well. If you have in mind a potion that will be swallowed by the patient, you should boil the water for several minutes to destroy any harmful bacteria—this will not affect the magical qualities of the potion. The water may look quite clean, but most witches will tell you that stored Moon water has a habit of getting a little green-tinged if it is left in the light or stored for a long time, so it makes sense to take steps to avoid this.

Now for your ingredients. If you are using herbal material, this should be gathered at the appropriate hour and Moon phase; if you are gathering it well in advance, it can then be dried and will keep for months in a cool, dark place until you are ready to use it. The plant material should then be chopped and placed in the water while it is hot, or even brought back to the boil, then left to steep while it cools. At this stage, enchantments can be added to the potion—if it is not for oral consumption—in the form of slips of paper with magical words and symbols on them in non-toxic, non-waterproof ink. Later, you can remove the soggy paper, knowing the enchantment itself has washed off into the potion. Leave it covered so that no more microbes can gain access. Crystals should only be added when the potion is cool, as otherwise they may split. Whether you are using herbs, crystals, spices, or all of these, the water can now be placed in a clear glass container that is tightly stoppered and left in moonlight overnight. Again, as with the Moon water, the potion can be succussed (towards the Moon if it is in the sky) to activate the ingredients, and after this it can be enchanted and used. It also never hurts to ask the deities you honour to bless the potion—and to thank Them afterwards.

Do take care not to use crystals that can be damaged by water, such as selenite, or that can be toxic, such as malachite, and obviously you will also have checked the properties of the herbs you are using before you gathered them! This also holds good if you are creating a potion for washing the skin or otherwise applying it externally: poisons can penetrate through the skin or cause rashes.

A little experimentation will show you which crystals you personally resonate with and which could benefit your health: a crystal tutor I once studied with told me to trust my judgment and choose the stones to which I was personally drawn because of their colour and lustre. This elixir can be made in larger quantities, stored (preferably in the dark), and used on a daily basis, perhaps just a drop or two on the tongue in the morning or just before going to bed. As with many healthy habits, it is better to do this at the same time every day and to make sure you do not miss a dose. You can also add it to your morning cup of tea or to a bowl of soup or just take it on a spoon like cough mixture. Some crystals, such as aquamarine, onyx, citrine, and garnet can greatly benefit the skin, and an elixir can be made from these, which can be dabbed on the face and neck before applying your normal moisturizer and foundation.

My own favourite Moon elixir varies according to my mood and the use to which I want to put it, but for boosting health and the sense of well-being, I would use rose quartz, clear quartz, sunstone, and lapis lazuli, while in an elixir intended for my skin, I might choose rose quartz (that's pretty well the alpha and omega of crystal therapy), citrine, and amethyst, as I have all these commoner crystals, and I trust them. If I am feeling stressed, tired, or nervous about something, I would reach for rose quartz, amethyst, tiger's eye, and green aventurine.

These crystal potions can also be diluted, without reducing their efficacy, just as homeopathic remedies are diluted down many times yet still retain their healing properties.

Animals and plants can also be helped by these potions, though in the case of animals it is probably better to stick to crystal elixirs, as they may refuse to drink potions made from plants, especially strong-smelling ones. A few drops of elixir on a sickly houseplant can achieve wonders, while crystals laid around the roots of a garden plant or shrub that obviously needs some TLC can also benefit it—the Moon elixir then occurs naturally without any further intervention from you!

Just a little bit about crystals worn on the person: many witches, and non-witches, habitually wear crystals chosen to benefit their health or their powers, or for protection, perhaps as beaded bracelets or a pendant with a single large crystal. Wearing these day in, day out will not harm them, but it never hurts to give them a clean and a boost. Washing them in warm, soapy water will achieve the first, but consider leaving them on your bedroom windowsill overnight, behind the curtains, to soak up the Moon's rays. You will find that they are all the better for it.

CHAKRAS

Eastern mysticism teaches that the body's structure includes many energy centres called chakras: there are over a hundred of these, not all of them within the body itself. The seven principal chakras run in a line from the crown of the head down through the spine to the base of the body, the bit you sit on, and each has its own set of correspondences and influences. These chakras are part of a network of meridians and lesser chakras throughout the body, which carry energy—prana or *chi*—along meridians, just as the physical system of veins and arteries carries blood with oxygen and nutrients to the organs. This is the basis for some Eastern medicine practices, including Reiki and acupuncture. If the chakras are blocked—not operating as they should—this can cause mental and physical health issues. Keeping the chakras well balanced and healthy involves keeping to a healthy diet, avoiding stress, and correct breathing (most of us breathe very inefficiently, not making full use of our lung capacity. Yoga and yogic breathing can correct this).

Most people can sense these chakras naturally, or once they have been taught their location, as they manifest as small points of greater sensitivity against the rest of the tissue with which they are surrounded. You may be aware, for example, of the chakra in the centre of your palm, or that between and slightly above the eyebrows, or the chakras along the soles of the feet.

Western mysticism has been quick to learn and adopt this idea, and magical and spiritual healing may make use of the chakras. A simple way to draw the Moon's healing into your body is by utilizing the seven main chakras.

Standing in full moonlight, strongly visualize the silvery healing light entering the crown chakra on the very top of your head and the chakra opening to draw it in (the chakras may be seen as little round windows or as many-petalled flowers). Allow the moonlight to infuse the chakra, which lights up with bright white light (some traditions state that this chakra is purple, and the one below it indigo).

Now draw the moonlight further down, to the chakra between your eyebrows, again, seeing it open and fill with light, this time purple. Repeat this drawing down into the throat chakra, which is blue; into the heart chakra, which is green; into the solar plexus, which is yellow; then the sacral chakra (level with the womb or the corresponding area in a man), which is orange; and finally the base chakra, which is red. Take your time over this, and enjoy any sensations you may feel. When all the chakras are opened and filled with light, take a deep breath and open your eyes: the exercise is over.

In many modern people, who perhaps lead stress-filled lives, take no exercise, eat a lot of unhealthy food, and drink too much alcohol and caffeine-filled drinks, the chakras can become unaligned, which can lead to more stress, dullness of spirit, and even physical illness if it goes on too long.

BALANCING AND CLEARING THE CHAKRAS

Exercises to balance and align the chakras include yoga and meditation, but this can also be done with careful intent and with the Moon's energies. Ideally, this should take a full lunation, as each chakra requires a different lunar energy. When the Moon is in the sky, you should sit at a window for these exercises so that the Moon is visible to you. If she is beneath the horizon, you can focus your intent on her position there.

Note: different websites and books will give you different phrases for each chakra, which can be very confusing. What I have listed here is what *I* feel to be right. If you do not agree with me, then use your own intuition or dowse with a pendulum to see what is right for you.

BASE CHAKRA

The base chakra is concerned more with physical life, and an imbalance in this chakra may manifest as an obsession with possessions and physical activities such as eating and drinking alcohol or smoking. You may feel insecure or possessive of your partner. You may experience difficulties around your appetites or your physical health generally.

Starting with the dark Moon, focus on your root or base chakra; it is helpful to light a red candle—the colour associated with this chakra—and perhaps have red textiles around you or a red scarf draped over the lightshade. Put on some soothing music for meditation and perhaps light some incense. Sit down: you do not need to assume the full Lotus position for these exercises, and if you find sitting on the ground difficult or uncomfortable, it is fine to sit in a chair. A hard-backed chair might be better than a squashy armchair, though, as you do not want to fall asleep during this exercise. Now focus on the Moon: this may be the most difficult phase of all—how do you visualize a dark Moon? It is helpful to simply envisage a black disc in the sky and to know in your heart of hearts that, although she is not visible, all her powerful lunar energies are still there and being emanated. Now state your intention, that you wish to balance and clear your base chakra. Say this calmly and firmly, as a fact that will manifest. Do some square breathing or other breathing exercises, whatever you normally do to calm down your mind and body, to bring you into a meditative state, and begin to turn your mind firmly towards the dark Moon. Focus on this dark disc. Feel the steady, throbbing rhythm of its darkness, where there are no needs, no hunger, no thirst, and no need to act in any way other than your own natural manner. Allow the warm, dark energies to enter your body and centre them on the base chakra. See the chakra as a spinning wheel—perhaps it is spinning too fast, and this is what has caused you to become unbalanced in your life. Perhaps it is too slow, which is why you have become sluggish, timid, and depressed. Allow the Moon energies to adjust the wheel until it is spinning correctly (you will recognize when this happens).

When you feel the balancing is complete, thank the Moon and open your eyes. You can check the chakra is now balanced by using a simple dowsing pendulum and simply asking it before letting it swing. If the pendulum swings in the direction agreed for "no" then you will need to repeat the exercise.

SACRAL CHAKRA

The sacral chakra, in your lower abdomen, relates to the new Moon: the very first sliver of Moon that you see in the sky in the evening, some days after the dark phase. This time, use orange colours around you and focus on your sexual energies. An underactive sacral chakra can result in a loss of interest in sex, a lack of energy and listlessness, and also possibly health issues affecting the lower organs in the body; while an overactive one can turn you into a manipulative, bossy, and possibly oversexed person.

Repeat the previous exercise, but this time focus on the new Moon, choosing a time from the night she first becomes visible until just before the first quarter (semicircle). State your intent. Pull her energies into the chakra as before, then check your results with a pendulum.

SOLAR PLEXUS CHAKRA

This chakra, in the pit of your stomach (where you feel "butterflies" if you are nervous or excited), relates to the first quarter of the Moon, and the exercise is very similar to the procedure for the base chakra. The colour correspondence is yellow. An unbalanced solar plexus chakra can lead to fearfulness, loss of confidence, and possible physical illness in the upper abdomen if it is underactive, or overconfidence, over-excitement, and aggression if it is overactive.

This is a phase that will easily be found in the sky in the early evening, so unless the night is overcast, you can focus on the real moonlight and repeat the exercise as before, drawing the energies into the chakra until you feel it has balanced. Again, check your pendulum.

HEART CHAKRA

The heart chakra relates to the second half of the waxing Moon, the gibbous phase that leads to the full, and the colour is green. An imbalance in this chakra affects your *feelings*, so that with an underactive chakra you may become a hard, selfish person lacking in compassion for others—or if the chakra is overactive, you may become weak, easily influenced, and overemotional.

Draw the Moon's energies into your heart—which you should feel quite strongly, as this chakra is very sensitive. Check your result with a pendulum afterwards.

THROAT CHAKRA

The throat chakra, which is located near your voice box, affects your ability to communicate, so that an underactive chakra will leave you unable to express yourself or to be creative, while an overactive one will cause you to become loud, talk too much, and often cause hurt to others without meaning to—being what some people I know would call "gobby". This chakra is associated with the full Moon and the days on either side of it, when the disc looks full, and with the colour blue. The technique is the same.

THIRD EYE CHAKRA

This chakra, between your brows, is of a higher vibration and, if underactive, can cause you to become sluggish, with a poor memory and less ability to make good decisions or think things through properly. If overactive, it can cause you to become exhausted by racing mental processes and the desire to make decisions for everyone. This chakra resonates with the colour purple and with the waning Moon, the first quarter after the full, the waning gibbous phase of the Moon—the phase that is larger than a semicircle with its whole, curved side pointing to the left.

CROWN CHAKRA

This final chakra is rather different and relates to your spiritual life, so it is unlikely that you would be aware of it being underactive or overactive. However, it is still a useful exercise to work on this chakra, which is on the very top of your head—where the ruler might rest when your mother was marking your height against the wardrobe when you were a child.

Meditating on this chakra can bring benefits in terms of your spiritual life and your connection with deity. It is associated with the colour white and with the last quarter, where the Moon is a waning crescent with her horns pointing to the right like a C.

One of the chakras is especially associated with the Moon and is particularly useful in maintaining health and the Bindu chakra is known as the Chandra chakra, or Moon chakra, and its symbol includes a white crescent Moon and 23 lotus petals. The centre is located just below the crown of the head at the back, in the area where your head might rest on a pillow if you were lying down, at the junction of the occipital and parietal bones of the skull (the occiput is the bowl-shaped base of the skull, and the parietal bones make up the sides and back of the skull—where you might wear a cap pushed back on your head). Some Reiki (a Japanese healing art) practitioners say that this chakra emits a silvery light like the Moon, and it is also thought that stimulating the chakra activates the pineal gland, which is underneath, to release hormones such as melatonin, which cause happiness and positivity, and thus help improve health. Melatonin is particularly important in the regulation of sleep cycles, so the importance of this minor chakra is obvious. Clearly it can play a role in fighting depression, exhaustion, and stress while boosting energy levels and good feelings of all kinds. Stimulating the chakra—and the gland beneath—may be as simple as pressing or rubbing on the correct spot with your finger or may involve yoga postures such as headstands or shoulder stands, while mudras—yogic postures involving only the hands—may also be employed, either on their own or as part of a whole-body yoga position.

The Bindu chakra offers many benefits in terms of health, but in these times of cheap and readily available junk food and eating disorders and obesity, one of the more important of these has to be its relationship with the appetites: stimulating the Bindu chakra can give the person more control over their appetite and even their sense of thirst, giving them the ability to turn away from unhealthy foods and alcoholic drinks.

CHAPTER TWELVE

The Spiritual Moon

"Enlightenment is like the Moon reflected on the water."
– Dogen Zenji

Looking up into the velvety night sky and into the glowing face of the full Moon and realizing that she is important in so many more ways than providing intermittent lighting at night is rather a "well, duh!" moment. The unearthly luminosity of the Moon awakens in many a sense of religious awe, or a feeling of close connection to nature, an awareness of the vastness of the universe and our own place in it. How could this object of amazing beauty fail to be of huge significance to anyone on a spiritual path? Maybe she was put there for this very reason.

Moonlight has all sorts of effects on the human mind, body, and spirit, including inducing calm, meditative moods, increasing your psychic ability, and awakening spiritual yearnings of all kinds. And all moods of moonlight have their own meanings and effects as well. For example, a lunar halo—where a ring of ice crystals in the Earth's atmosphere creates a pale ring around the Moon—is seen in many traditions as a spiritual message of hope, of enlightenment, of the presence of God. These phenomena are believed to be a message from the universe, reminding us of our connection to the divine and urging us to focus on our spiritual growth and development. One quite basic ingredient is that moonlight is a nocturnal phenomenon: at night we often feel closer to our deities, more involved with our spiritual sides, and, of course, night is generally a time of silence, peace, and privacy as others are in bed or shut inside their homes watching TV.

Moving into a closer relationship with the Moon is beneficial in all sorts of ways and can give a structure and reality to your spiritual life that can only improve your journey. The Moon is your friend when it comes to travel on your spiritual path, lighting your way like an enormous spiritual lantern—even when you cannot see her. Priests, shamans, and other spiritual practitioners have long been aware of this and have made use of the Moon and her phases to benefit themselves and those who seek their wisdom.

Simply using moonlight for your meditation sessions is very helpful, as the Moon's rays deliver a calming, soothing energy that assists the mind in its journey from full consciousness to altered mind states—and helps suppress the mental chatter meditators call "monkey mind". Mental and spiritual growth are both encouraged.

As we have seen, Wiccans and other pagans are wont to clarify their intentions and begin new work of all kinds at the new Moon while keeping other phases for different work. In the same way, shamanic practitioners will use the new and full phases for ceremonies, initiations, blessings, healing, and astral journeying. The new Moon particularly might be used for purifying ceremonies such as a sweat lodge, which can be as gruelling as it sounds, and is a method for cleansing the body and spirit (see aura cleansing below). They believe that the Moon can intensify emotions or bring buried emotions, anxieties, and fears to the surface where they can be addressed with healing and releasing rituals.

Defining shamanism can be tricky: elements of it are common in many pagan spiritualities in the form of meditations, pathworkings, and journeying—whatever name is given to it—and some people are capable of regular astral travel. In other practices, shamanic practitioners may "shapeshift". Many shamanic practices involve chanting or drumming to alter brainwave patterns and assist the practitioner in achieving travel, or they may include the use of plant drugs such as ayahuasca or mescaline to alter consciousness. These journeys, which may involve collaborating with spirit guides, ancestors, and other spirits along the way, can be used to heal others, release negative influences, benefit situations, or simply progress the practitioner on their own spiritual journey. Shamanic practice may even include seemingly impossible feats like yogic flight (a sort of leap or hop made from the lotus position) or walking barefoot on hot coals, made possible by the alteration of the mental state of the participants.

As we saw in previous chapters, many practitioners make use of the energy centres called *chakras* in the human body, and often pagan rituals include a small ritual to open the chakras. Often these are very stylized and poetic and may not be recognized for what they are.

The simple ritual to close the chakras given in Chapter Ten matches a similar procedure to open them before any spiritual work, prayers, or worship generally. Just as with the closing, you can see your whole body as a house of several stories, with windows that need to be opened, or you can see the chakras as flowers, opening their petals, or coloured wheels spinning open—whatever works for you.

As we saw in the last chapter, a lesser but still remarkable chakra called the Bindu, which is influenced by the Moon and sometimes called the Moon Centre, is very important in maintaining health and well-being. And the Bindu can also help with spiritual matters, including your daily meditation routine. Using the Moon mudra associated with this chakra will also bring benefits, amplifying the use of the chakra by stimulation in the physical yoga poses. The Moon mudra involves sitting in a relaxed but upright position in a chair or on the floor and using controlled, slow breathing to create a meditative mood. The person places the right hand on top of the left, with the palms facing down and the hands pointing in opposite directions, the left with its fingers pointing to the right and the right with its fingers pointing left, while the thumbs are pointed towards the stomach with their tips touching, so that they form a triangle. The mantra "Sat naam" (which means "I am the truth") can be chanted or meditated upon, or alternatively the mantra "Amritam" ("I am immortal") can be used.

Also located on the head, the occipital chakra, also known as the occipital lobe chakra or zeal chakra, is influenced by the Moon and deals with dreams and the ability to recall dreams, astral travel, intuition, and clairvoyance—all the "territory" of the Moon—and with communicating with spirit guides. This centre is found at the very base of the skull at the back, just above where the spinal cord enters the skull (you can feel a hollow path leading to a small bony protuberance in this area). It works closely with the medulla chakra, at the base of the brain.

So how can spiritual seekers use the phases of the Moon to further their spiritual practices? Here are a few helpful hints on choosing the right time for the right activity.

New. Perhaps the best way of using the new Moon is just as a launch pad for a new project, such as starting a new regime of meditation, yoga, or prayer. Most spiritual people (and people on less spiritual quests, such as dieting, quitting smoking, or giving up bad habits generally) are familiar with the cycle of the enthusiastic new start, followed by neglect and laziness, followed by renewed resolutions that go with our hopes of improving ourselves mentally, physically, and spiritually. It doesn't always work out, does it? Often the world and life get in the way—or we allow them to. It is easy to beat yourself up about these failures, but almost everyone experiences them, and you have to cut yourself some slack...It wasn't meant to be that easy, or it would be worthless. However, we generally find that once a habit—such as rising a little early to meditate or making the time for prayer before sleeping—is established, we become better at keeping to our goals. Some psychologists believe that it takes a month—or one lunation—to form a new habit (or perhaps to break an old one). Though others state that this may take much longer or would have to be calculated in terms of *repetitions* rather than time, a lunation is still a useful time for addressing one's aspirations towards self-improvement and development. Once formed, the habit will be quite strongly binding—experts estimate that up to 43% of all daily behaviours are driven by habit, to the extent that the person performing them may hardly even be aware of them.

Beginning a new spiritual journey at the new Moon is therefore psychologically sound advice: we humans are made to see boundaries, endings, and new beginnings as significant, and whether this is a new Moon, or New Year's Day, or the first day of the month, or simply Monday morning, taking up a new spiritual practice, or reviving a neglected old one, is given a psychological boost by this timing.

Make a little ceremony of this: light a candle and some incense, and observe the actual moment of the new Moon (to be found in an ephemeris or much more easily on various websites—though be aware that these sometimes give times for other countries, so you need to be sure you have the timings appropriate for your location). For projects using other phases,

I would recommend sitting where you can view the Moon, but of course this is not possible at the new, as it is invisible. State your intention or write it in your journal, and begin your meditation (or other spiritual project) straight away. For experienced practitioners, they might also sit at their altar and perhaps have symbols of new beginnings around them, such as the Norse rune Berkana and The Fool Tarot card.

If you are marking something especially important and significant to you, you could start with a Moon bath to cleanse and prepare yourself. This cannot be done at the new Moon, of course, but can be done on any night when the Moon can actually be seen. Moon bathing is an ancient practice that continues today among spiritual seekers and can be as simple as sitting outside under the light of the Moon—obviously a full Moon works best—for as long as you like (no danger of moonburn!). If you don't have a garden or other space where you can safely sit at night, it can be done just as easily in front of a window, with you sitting facing the Moon. Light some incense and a candle or two, put on some dreamy meditation music, then just relax and absorb the magical light, which should bring about a light meditative state, leaving you feeling refreshed, relaxed, and at peace with everyone and everything. Obviously, being skyclad (nude) for this is ideal, but that rather depends on where your window faces and the degree of privacy you can expect. A Moon bath can also involve water, to which you can add herbs, salt, crystals, and oils (be careful when using essential oils in a modern plastic bath, as they can damage the finish). If your bathroom window faces the Moon, so much the better, but if it does not, you can place items around the bath to capture the essence of the Moon: little mirrors, certain Moon crystals like selenite (don't get it wet, as it will dissolve!), moonstone, white quartz, and aquamarine. If possible, use natural water in your bath, especially if you live in a town where a lot of chlorination is added to the water supply; and if you have made Moon water (see previous chapter) then it is a no-brainer to add some of this to the bath. Again, light incense and candles and turn out the main lights, put on some good meditation or other soothing music, and enjoy a long, luxurious soak with your mind firmly in neutral gear. This is a wonderful exercise before anything important, and this includes pagan initiations and other rituals. It is also a good exercise to dispel negativity. If this sounds cuckoo to you, that warm water can wash away energies and spiritual qualities; then just remember that the first port of call for a technician exposed to harmful radiation is a simple old-fashioned shower!

Waxing. Once the Moon is three or four days past the full, she ceases to have those vibrant, brand-new energies and settles down into more rounded, developing, ripening energies. This is the time to consolidate the work you started anew. If you have, for example, started a new meditation *habit*, then be mindful during this phase, stick to your plans, and carry them through, as deliberate adherence to your new routine will pay off in the form of a created habit that will serve you later on. It is too easy to start a new regime, congratulate yourself on this initiative and the willpower it took to start it, then go ahead and forget about it three days out of four. I know—I've been there! The waxing is the phase when you will need to put the most work in to maintain and consolidate the project ... but it does get easier. By the time the full Moon arrives, you should find that you are getting into the good habit already and, if something happens to prevent you, then you are aware and regretful, rather than oblivious.

Remember, this phase and the full Moon represent the Mother aspect of the Goddess, the all-fertile, all-nurturing

Creatrix, so projects involving creativity should be suitable for this phase. Spiritual journaling can be a very big help on your path, and while you might start this practice at the new phase, setting your intentions and identifying new beginnings, it is the energies of the waxing one that will really get your creative juices flowing. Journaling is something you do for yourself: the journal is not meant to be seen by anyone else but yourself and the Gods, so you can write your truest, inmost thoughts and feelings in it, your deepest secrets. As with a *Book of Shadows*, this can be kept in any format, even on your computer, but is more satisfying and perhaps works better if you use your own creativity to embellish it and make it special. While a few lines about what you have learned through an argument with your partner or a difficulty at work might keep you reminded, you can also use your own artwork to not only decorate the pages and look special but also to exorcise problems, celebrate achievements, and pick out and underline the entries you consider the most meaningful to you in terms of your development and attainment.

Full. I could go on for pages about the use of this phase! The full is suitable for many different kinds of magic but also for spiritual purposes. Cleanse your magical tools, your crystals, runes, and Tarot cards in the light of the full Moon. Her silvery light will wash away any negative vibes that may have stuck to your tools and repersonalize them for your own use. This is especially important if your tools are shared by others: as a coven high priestess, I tend to let others handle my tools, even my athame, during ritual (there isn't always room on the altar for everyone's athames, and some people may not remember or wish to bring theirs). Obviously, you would not let your intimate magical artefacts be handled by just anyone, but members of your coven are, or should be, like close kin, or it may happen accidentally if a visitor to your home picks up a magical tool out of curiosity before you have had time to warn him or her not to touch. In either case, the tools may need cleaning afterwards, so that they become your own special tools again. I have personally observed that the shiny tools, such as the athame and the white-handled knife, and even the cup, if it is made of metal, can acquire a dull patina through use, and that cleansing in this way can leave them brighter and cleaner-looking—even though no physical cleaning has been done.

Choose the full Moon for working through a problem: let that brilliant light illuminate exactly what it is you are up against and what you hope to achieve. Bring the work to a climax at the moment of full, and then break down your circle—or whatever you set up to perform the work—and go to bed. By the next quarter, you will be pretty sure to see some progress towards your goal.

Due to the powerful, surging properties of full Moon energies, this phase can also be used for projects that need a little turbocharging, and this is especially true of rituals involving family. People become estranged in the best of families, due not just to disagreements but to geographical distance and busy lives and illness, and all sorts of other reasons. Due to the strength of human emotions involved, this kind of magic is difficult, but full Moon energies will give you more bang for your buck and make it more likely that this magical reaching out will succeed. Again, I am reminded of that nursery rhyme: *"I see the Moon, the Moon sees me, the Moon sees somebody that I want to see ..."*—actually quite an ideal little enchantment (intention-setting chant) for such work.

Many practitioners will tell you that spiritual practices like prayer and meditation work better at the full. This is not to say that this is the only time you should perform them, but it may be beneficial to make a point of performing them with mindfulness at the full, perhaps setting up your space in a more formal way than you would normally, with candles, incense, sacred pictures, and music.

Waning. The waning phases of the Moon are suitable for magic concerning banishing and reducing problems, but also for honouring the ancestors. You might get a flash of someone in skins holding a flint-headed spear, but your ancestors are everyone who has contributed to making you who you are. They are your parents, your grandparents, your aunts and uncles, and all the family you can remember from your past, plus many that you can't. These are your ancestors of blood (plus any step-parents or other relatives by adoption or marriage), but you also have ancestors of other kinds. Ancestors can also be anyone who was an influence on you, who mentored you, or helped you to learn a skill or gain confidence. In spiritual matters, we have ancestors of *tradition* as well—maybe your high priestess or your grove mother if you are a pagan, or perhaps the people who founded your belief stream, such as the Buddha, or Mohammed, or in pagan belief Ross Nichols, the founder of the Order of Bards, Ovates and Druids (OBOD), or Gerald Gardner, the father of Wicca. In initiatory pagan streams, ancestors will also include the person who initiated you and those who initiated him or her before that. Ancestors of place might be the people who lived in your house many years before you, or the people who inhabited your region in the distant past, and whose spirits and languages perhaps live on in the area; you may or may not share DNA with them, but you are walking in their footsteps, seeing the landscapes that they used to see, maybe even living in their houses, or where their houses used to be, or doing the jobs they used to do.

THE SPIRITUAL MOON

You may feel drawn to remembering your ancestors at the waning Moon, whether it is a prayer for your aunt who has just passed away, or your parents and grandparents, or any of the types of ancestors mentioned above. While you may remember them at certain anniversaries, such as their birthday or the day they died, a monthly observance at the waning Moon is a beautiful way to keep their memory alive throughout the year. An easy way to honour them is to create a permanent or semi-permanent space for them, perhaps on a dresser or shelf, on which you can place photographs and other memorabilia, along with flowers, candles, and crystals. At some phase of the waning Moon, perhaps just after the full, tend this family shrine, perhaps taking off all the photos and objects and giving the space a good clean with wax or spray polish, dusting the items, and perhaps renewing any flowers that have gone past their best. By doing this you are following in the footsteps of countless people in the past who kept shrines to their beloved dead, as well as to the deities they honoured. Not everyone feels comfortable praying, especially aloud, but you may feel a simple greeting to the people remembered, perhaps by lifting their photo and looking at it; or even placing a kiss on the frame if it was someone to whom you were especially close, is just as respectful.

In the previous chapter, we looked at the preparation of Moon elixirs for health, healing, and beauty, and of course these also have their place in ritual and religious practice. My coven commonly uses Moon water, from a glass bowl left under the light of the full Moon overnight, for circle casting; and for special occasions, a Moon elixir could certainly be substituted. But why stop there?

Perhaps you have a magical working that needs to be performed at the new Moon or at some other phase. With a little forethought, you can create Moon phase elixirs for every phase of the Moon except the dark phase. If the Moon is in the sky and visible, the container of water can be left below it, and some of the fuller phases will produce enough light to demonstrate that they are hitting the liquid. With some of the others, careful and regular succussion (see Chapter Ten), accompanied by visualizing the Moon phase and seeing its light entering the liquid, can encourage the Moon's energies into the elixir.

CLEANSING THE AURA

The aura is not a discrete appendage to a living being but a sort of glowing penumbra—visible to some people—a field manifested by the energies and emotions flowing through the person or other living being (even trees and plants have auras). In a happy, healthy, and positive person, the aura will be full of bright, attractive colours; while in a depressed, selfish, angry, or otherwise negative person, it will be dull and dark, with livid colours. The colours are usually a mixture and may remain largely unchanged throughout a person's lifetime, but usually they change as the person changes, reflecting the different moods.

Put simply, your aura reflects how you are feeling. But it is also possible to cleanse and brighten the aura—and your mind and spirit at the same time—with an aura cleansing.

A first—and rather obvious—step is a health check. There's nothing like feeling unwell to lower your spirits and your mood, annihilate your energy, and consequently muddy your aura. If you have a nasty cold, a toothache, a sprained foot ... or any annoying minor condition then you should take time to sort this out (or see a dentist!) before you can really achieve anything with your aura. Maybe see your doctor if you are generally out of sorts, and check that you don't maybe have a health condition that needs sorting. If you already have a known health problem, there is still a lot you can do to improve things.

Now examine your mental health. Is there some reason you are feeling grumpy, depressed, angry, sad, or mentally lethargic? Perhaps your relationship has run into trouble, or you are in a job that you hate, or someone close to you has been unkind and hurt your feelings? Again, address this situation if you can; but if you can't, you can still do quite a lot to brighten things and cleanse your aura.

The first port of call should always be a Moon bath or at least a shower. Use lots of your favourite scented bath products, and include salt and cleansing herbs, tied into a muslin square, and your favourite crystals (just having these with you in the shower cubicle is enough, or you can pop them inside your shower cap—be careful when you take it off though, and don't drop them all!). Don't just wash dirt from your body: visualize the grubbiness and grime from inside your spirit being washed away and going down the drain—see it as actual physical dirt.

Meditation and breathing exercises are an excellent way of cleansing the aura, and the Moon can be invoked for this as well.

Sit in a comfortable chair, face the window and, if possible, the rising Moon. If the Moon is not in the sky, then just visualize her—she is there somewhere! Perhaps imagine yourself sitting on a moonlit beach overlooking the sea and seeing the Moon rise as a gigantic silver ball over the sea. Feel her energies surrounding you. Now imagine drawing the glorious silver light of the Moon into your body with a long, deep breath. Try to feel it entering your lungs, like wine in your mouth, going into your bloodstream and passing into and through every part of your body. Imagine, as you breathe out, that dark and dirty air is leaving your body; all the negativity is flooding out, displaced by the magical moonlight.

Continue breathing in this way for as long as you need to. The exercise will be enhanced by the addition of soothing meditation music, well-chosen incense and, of course, the inclusion of your favourite crystals.

This exercise can be carried out almost anywhere: on the bus to work, sitting at your desk, even in your armchair as other members of the family watch TV, but of course it will work best when you have a degree of privacy.

SPIRITUAL REAWAKENING

Most people who follow a religion seriously have experienced periods like this: when they feel that the Ancient Ones (or whoever they see as their deity) have vanished from the landscape, that anything they do is pointless, that everything they believe in has turned out to be moonshine and fairytales, and they might as well go and get a job in the Inland Revenue office and tick the "atheist" box on the next census form.

Discovering the Ancient Ones is an amazing and beautiful experience ... suddenly we see everything in brighter colours, everyone is smiling, mysterious signs pop out at us from every side, and we know mysteries of which mere mortals do not dream. This is called falling in love, and it happens to pairs of human beings, as well as Wiccans (and Christians, Hindus, Muslims, Jews, Sikhs, etc.), when we first discover how amazing She/He is and that we have found our true path. And it does feel just like that hearts and flowers sensation we get when we are in love with another person.

But it can't last ... we would burn out. And, as with human relationships, if we are lucky, it turns into something truer, more meaningful, and less soaked in hormones. And the

Goddess and God know this, and They don't really have an interest in keeping us drooling and cross-eyed with puppy love for Them ... They want us to evolve because that's what life is for. So, we have times when we can't connect with Them, when They feel so distant that we begin to doubt Their existence, to wonder whether we imagined the whole experience of meeting Them for the first time. It is painful, it is depressing, and it can lead to some people, whose faith is not strong, abandoning their spiritual practice altogether.

But there is another secret that They know, and some more experienced worshippers (in any faith) share: more progress is made during times of spiritual dryness—as long as the worshipper keeps the faith.

If you come to your altar every day and go through the motions of tending it, of lighting candles, placing flowers, and praying, even if it all seems empty to you, then you are moving along your path, perhaps even faster than you were when everything seemed beautiful and easy. We are creatures of earth as well as spirit, and we have cycles that inform every part of our lives. Old married people know this: I love my husband and have for 50 years, but I know that marriages go up and down in just this way, while many newlyweds have floundered because they did not know this and assumed that at the first quarrel the spark had just gone and the whole relationship had turned to ashes. Worship must be a cerebral activity as well as an emotional one; in fact, the purposeful enactment of prayer and ritual is more important in the long run than the emotional responses this evokes in us.

So lighting that candle, dusting the altar, speaking the words, and making the gestures will have an effect ... And the cycle will turn again as it always does. Only, this time, you will know it and be stronger for it, and the presence of the Lord and Lady will be all the sweeter for it.

And what does this have to do with the Moon, you ask? Quite a lot: the Moon is at the heart of so much that we do in paganism, like a power station sitting in the heart of a populated area: without it, how many cheerful lighted windows, how many tempting shop displays, how many street lamps, and how many safely lit pedestrian crossings would we see?

Your first port of call should be a Moon bath, either sitting nude in full moonlight or, if that is not currently possible, a bath in warm water with Moon water and crystals added. Bathe yourself mindfully, imagining all your spiritual blockages being rinsed away by the power of the water and its ingredients. Now rise from the bath, dry yourself, and put on whatever you normally wear for magic or spiritual work and go to your altar.

It will be helpful if you repeat this ritual bathing at each quarter of the Moon, but it is also necessary to stick to your spiritual duties; else your spiritual life may be in danger of fizzling out altogether. Even if it all feels pointless and hopeless, even if you would rather be watching *Strictly*—DO IT. Light the candle, make the gestures, speak the words. Think for a moment of the clichéd elderly Catholic woman, kneeling before her crucifix and saying a Hail Mary: she knows what she is doing. Do not despise this kind of habit, for it has real value, even if it seems like corny and meaningless repetition at first.

If you do not already keep a journal, now is a very good time to start: keep tabs on your activities at the various Moon phases, noting every step forward (and those that go back), and you will see a promising pattern emerging, and before too long you should be enjoying your relationship with deity as you did before. Only this time, you are armed with the knowledge that a hiccup like this one is not permanent.

CHAPTER THIRTEEN

Bringing the Moon into Your Practice

"Everyone is a moon, and has a dark side he never shows to anybody."

– Mark Twain

Once you start to discover the Moon and what she can do for you, you will want her influence in your magical and spiritual life in all sorts of ways. You might just toss out your old bolline (magical knife), which has served you well for decades, in favour of a crescent-shaped one, or spend happy hours carving, painting, or poker-working Moon symbols onto all your altar tools (the Craft has this effect on many people: you might be rubbish at *craft*, but if you need something for your *Craft*, that's a different matter, and you find your hitherto clumsy hands making and creating things you never knew they could achieve!). Whole new worlds open up to you as you discover you can also create brand-new items, mindfully and with the appropriate materials and symbols: Moon wand, anyone? As any witch will tell you, your magical tools and materials will be all the more powerful and meaningful to you if you have made them yourself. A slightly wonky candle with herbs in its wax, molded in an old yogurt tub and carved with symbols by your own fair hand, will give you more bang for your buck than an expensive candle bought at a store (and doubtless full of chemicals); and your own incense, mixed from herbs that you have grown and dried yourself, may not be as sweet to the nose as something from your local magic shop, but it will give you more *magic,* not to mention pride in what you do.

Let us take a look at one of the principal items witches use: the magic potion. If you want to bring as much of the Moon's energies into this as you can, than the work may have to start weeks or even months before you need the potion (remember Cerridwen, with her cauldron boiling away for a year and a day?).

The first thing you need is a good book explaining which herbs, spices, and wild plants are ruled by the Moon. There are plenty of these on the market, and you can still buy Culpeper's seminal work of 1653, *The Complete Herbal,* which, in line with beliefs at the time and conveniently for us witches, gives the planetary and elemental rulers of all the plants he describes. His line drawings leave a lot to be desired, to modern eyes at least, but once you have the proper name and Latin classification of an herb, you can Google it for a perfect identification photo.

Many wildflowers are protected and should never be picked, while others should not be picked to their destruction; i.e. dug up, roots and all. Never, whatever the plant, take every bit of it from its site; leave some to grow back and reproduce so it is there in the future for you and others. Ideally the plant material should be gathered in dry weather; as if it is wet then it may rot rather than dry (if plants are very dusty, you may need to wash them when you get them home, but be very careful to pat them dry with paper towels and lay them out in a single layer to dry—if you have one, a domestic dehumidifier is excellent for this purpose and will dry a tray of herbs placed

BRINGING THE MOON INTO YOUR PRACTICE

near it in hours). You do not need any special equipment: most plants will dry perfectly well hung in well-spaced bunches in the kitchen or the garden shed, away from direct light. Alternatively, you can freeze them in ice-cube trays or place them in jars and cover them with oil. In the latter case, the oil takes on the aroma, colour, and magical influence of the herbs and becomes an additional substance you can use magically.

A quick look online will help you identify most wild plants, and others can be grown in your garden or bought as cooking ingredients—but more important is the Moon's involvement. If possible, pick leaves and flowers in the light of the full Moon—bearing in mind that this must be done before the instant of fullness, as the energies then change over to waning Moon energies (although, as discussed in previous chapters, if you need materials for a banishing spell or a spell of new beginnings or any spell that uses energies of other phases, pick the plants at the appropriate phase). Gather them *mindfully*, perhaps enchanting them with your own words as you do so, imbuing them with the intentions of your spell. For a Moon spell, you will ideally need to keep to Moon numbers, that is, three or nine types of herbs. These magical numbers go beyond Moon magic and can be adhered to for many potions.

Here below is the recipe for one of the most famous herbal potions of all, the tenth-century *Nine Herbs Charm*, which was used against snakebite and other poisons but has many uses in magic, including the anointing and consecration of your rune set and other tools.

The charm is in the form of a long verse which mentions nine herbs:

- Betony *(Stachys officinalis)* is a striking, purple-flowered member of the mint family found in hedgerows and flower meadows.

- Crab apple *(Malus sylvestris)*. It is common to find this shrubby tree, with its tiny, hard, sour fruits in rural hedgerows, and the fruits were once gathered—and still are by foraging enthusiasts—to make crab apple jelly and other preserves.
- Fennel *(Foeniculum vulgare)*, with its onion-shaped bulb, aniseed aroma and feathery greenery, is available in most supermarkets, or you may grow it yourself, as it is useful in the kitchen.
- Lamb's cress *(Cardamine hirsuta)*. This gorgeous little plant is probably growing in your garden path right now, like a bright green lace doily or a living mandala. It is slightly more problematic to dry as, like culinary cress, it is somewhat fleshy.
- Mayweed *(Matricaria spp.)*. Again, this member of the chamomile family is probably growing on your path. A very common weed, it has delicate, feathery leaves, white and yellow daisy-like flowers with a protuberant disc floret, and a characteristic "pineapple" scent.
- Mugwort *(Artemisia vulgaris)*, an important herb in any witch's cupboard, is common, easy to find and easy to dry. It is not difficult to spot at night on the roadside, as its silvery foliage seems to light up brilliant white in car headlights.
- Plantain *(Plantago spp.)* is common in lawns and the bane of gardeners. It forms a tough rosette of round or longish leaves with long parallel veins, and from this grow the characteristic green or brown hairy-looking seed heads, which look like little draught excluders.
- Stinging nettle *(Urtica dioica)*. You should have no problems finding this one!
- Thyme *(Thymus vulgaris)* is a common kitchen herb and, if you do not have it in your garden, it is available in all supermarkets.

You will note that none of these are Moon herbs, but were associated with Odin (who aligns with Mercury in correspondences)—but it is an example of how you can plan an herbal potion. Do not forget that your store cupboard can also be very useful, as those little jars of dried spices and herbs you bought to make a casserole or a curry will likely have a magical use also, and fresh items bought from the greengrocer as well: Moon items include lemons, which many people might have hanging around in their fridge (especially after a drinks party!), and you can carefully peel the outer zest from these and dry it, or just freeze the whole fruit in slices for magical use later on. Ah, but what about picking them at the correct lunar hour, I hear you ask? There's not going to be any information on the label regarding at which Moon phase these herbs and fruit were gathered! Let me share a little secret: you can succuss dried herbs and frozen plant matter in their containers under the appropriate Moon phase, in the same way you succussed the Moon water. This revives it to the instant it is magically struck and brings the lunar energies of that moment into it.

ESSENTIAL OILS

When in doubt, reach for the oil bottle. Fact: essential oils are expensive and sometimes difficult to obtain. Also fact: they can last for years if kept in a cool, dark place, they come in tiny bottles that are easily stored in a small space and can even be carried with you in a small case, they have all the virtues of fresh herbs (except that you cannot take them orally), they smell wonderful and they can be used in one of those ceramic oil burners where, unlike smoking incense, they will benefit people with breathing issues such as asthma, instead of making them unwell.

Some essential oils ruled by the Moon are:

- Coconut
- Eucalyptus
- Frankincense
- Jasmine
- Lemon (also lemon balm and lemon grass)
- Lotus
- Myrrh
- Rose
- Sandalwood

You will note that there are nine oils listed here, so you can create your own lunar version of a nine herbs/oils potion. For a very special ritual or piece of Moon magic, why not use an oil blend of three or nine oils in an oil burner instead of incense? If you prefer incense, it is also very easy to make your own, though collecting and drying the materials does take some time. Remember: an incense blend does not have to include 100% aromatics, as some of the plants will contribute their magical influence, rather than a pleasant scent, and they may not smell any more fragrant than burning paper. One or two aromatic herbs or resins (which can be bought online or from a magic shop) are all you need in the mix for a pleasant or magical aroma.

MOON TOOLS

The centre of any ritual—and of many magical workings too—is the altar. Whether this is your coffee table, with a special cloth laid over it for witchy work, or an impressive piece of carved oaken furniture kept exclusively for magic and ritual, it can still be "mooned up". If it is not too large a piece, it can be moved outside and left to be bathed in moonlight at the full, if the weather is dry. It can also be anointed with Moon-based potions (it can also be cleaned with Moon water) and, if it is an altar and not a family table, it can also be decorated with lunar symbols and crystals. Inanimate items retain a memory of what they have been used for, which accounts for the haunted pieces of furniture you occasionally hear about, so treating a table or chest as special in itself will help to consecrate it and imbue it with the energies you need for your work.

Many shop-bought wands, athames, and cauldrons, not to mention smaller altar items such as libation bowls and candle holders, already have Moon symbols on them. This is very encouraging when you are starting out in your Craft and don't really know how to go about the creation of your tools. In some cases, this is the route to take: who can create an athame (witch's ritual knife) from scratch unless they are prepared to take blacksmithing courses? However, if you are a coven neophyte, your high priestess will hopefully have instructed you to make as many as possible yourself, as part of your training; and even solitaries can find this advice in books and on websites. But it doesn't have to be very challenging. Some items cannot be made from scratch by the average witch, but they can be personalized and decorated. I started out with a kitchen boning knife as my athame, very many years ago, as there were no helpful High Street magic shops in those days, then I graduated to a shop-bought athame with a pentacle set in the hilt, but ... I suppose because I had had no part in its design or decoration, it didn't really hit the spot. Then, one day, I saw a hunting knife on display—plain and without so much as a pentagram label hanging off it. I knew it as soon as I saw it, and this is an experience many of you will have, this *recognition*. The shop owner sold it to me cheap because it had been in the cabinet a while and had slight marks on the blade (which I soon scrubbed off), and I bore it home in triumph, as the saying goes. I bought an electric engraving tool, watched a few YouTube videos, then took my courage in both hands and engraved it: a pentacle on one side of the ricasso (the flat bit at the handle end of the blade) and my own personal bindrune on the other. The secret to doing this is to have your design on a piece of paper, which you glue to the metal surface, then use the tool over and through the paper, which can then be soaked and scrubbed off. This stops the tool from skidding around on the smooth metal and creating a messy line instead of a crisp one. I had never done this before, but I was delighted with the result ... because *I had done it myself!*

Many witches, in addition to personalizing their athame with decorations, also give it a name, and other tools may be given names as well. The thinking behind this is that it binds the tool to the witch and gives it more *importance,* more power.

Painting, carving, or poker-working a crescent Moon onto a knife is a great deal easier than creating a pentagram by the same methods; and when painting, you can also use a stencil to make it even easier, as the pentagram is a difficult geometric shape that looks very odd if you are out by even a degree on one of the angles. A crescent Moon executed in silver enamel—some of these craft enamels have sparkle as well—on the hilt of a knife can look spectacular. While creating it, be aware of the difference between a waxing and a waning crescent, as you will want one or the other on your tools, depending on what kind of magic you do.

Creating a wand involves more choices, as you will want to consider the very wood you use for it. The most obvious choice is willow, but any white wood will also be suitable and look beautiful. If you take wood from a living tree, it is traditional to ask the tree's permission and to leave a small gift behind in return. But with councils hacking down hedges every autumn, you may not need to cut the wood yourself. The next decision is whether to strip off the bark or leave it *au naturel*. If the bark is left, then you should bear in mind that it will dull and darken in colour with age as it dries—although it can also be incised, cutting through to the wood beneath to create symbols. Then comes the decoration. A quick look on Google will show you wands tarted up with copper wire and all sorts of accessories, but this is just not necessary. All the wand needs is your *respect*, your mindfulness as you create it, and your knowledge that it will be special to you and bring something to your magic and ritual. By all means, cover it from base to tip in Moon symbols, glitter, and white crystals, but it does not need this. My own wand—though I have a pot full of twisty, wired, and crystally ones that I have been given over the years—is a simple length of straight branch cut from an ash tree and with its bark still on, poker-worked with runes, and then given a light coat of acrylic because I prefer a bit of a shine. It's mine; I made it, and I love it, simple as it is. Of course, these ideas can also transfer to a besom, which is another item most witches like to have. The choice of willow or other white wood, some woody Moon herbs in the bristle end, and some lunar decoration, perhaps with some crystals wired to the handle, can make your broom into a lunar broom.

One of the biggest and showiest items on your altar will probably be the cauldron in which you mix herbal and crystal potions and burn incense or papers with spells. This can be anything from a small, roughly cauldron-shaped ceramic pot to a full-sized cast iron monster on three legs, big enough to cook a turkey in. The cauldron is a natural Moon accessory, as it is connected with the Moon Goddess Cerridwen, as well as being an iconic artefact associated with witchcraft since time immemorial.

A cauldron can be dedicated to the Moon with a small ritual, which should be undertaken outdoors, preferably under the full Moon. Give the vessel a good cleanse first with saltwater and maybe some sage smoke and a good physical polish to make it as shiny as possible (not all cauldrons shine, but it should be as clean as you can get it). The words you say are your own choice, but a simple, "I dedicate this cauldron to the Moon and to the magic of the Moon," will suffice while holding the cauldron up to the light of the Moon. After the words of dedication, light a white or silver candle and stand it in the cauldron. Remember: always perform these actions *mindfully*. Your purpose should be in the front of your mind the whole time. Thank the Moon or whichever lunar Goddess you invoked, and leave the candle outdoors in the cauldron to burn down. This will need cleaning out the next morning—although modern candles do not leave a great deal of residue—after which, you should use your cauldron regularly as a vessel for making Moon water.

ACKNOWLEDGING THE MOON

I remember once reading in some chick-lit novel about a wild, witchy girl who kept unwanted pregnancies at bay by her use of herbs and by *curtseying* to the Moon. Once, long ago, our ancestors would have understood this concept, for they would have acknowledged the Moon as a deity every time they saw her. The old Irish superstition says that it is bad luck to see the new Moon for the first time through a glass window; that you should be careful to spot her only when you are out of doors, when you should see her over your right shoulder.

I cannot really offer you any advice on this concept at all: if you are meant to be a Moon priest or a Moon witch, or to use the Moon in your rites and magic, then you will find yourself doing it naturally. You will find that you *know* when the Moon is in the sky, that you will know without more than a moment's thought what phase she is in; and often you will feel drawn, called, to the outdoors at night to walk under her light and commune with her. In return, she will make her magic powers available to you, for she has plenty for everyone. Go on ... get out there and get to *know* her!

www.ingramcontent.com/pod-product-compliance
Lightning Source LLC
Chambersburg PA
CBHW070756100426
42742CB00012B/2153